LAST WORDS

FINAL

THOUGHTS

OF CATHOLIC

SAINTS &

SINNERS

PAUL THIGPEN

SERVANT
BOOKS

PUBLISHED BY ST. ANTHONY MESSENGER PRESS
CINCINNATI, OHIO

Cover design: Candle Light Studios
Cover image: Photodisc/Brent Vegisir
Book design: Mark Sullivan

LIBRARY OF CONGRESS CATALOGING-IN-PUBLICATION DATA

Thigpen, Paul.
  Last words of Catholic saints and sinners, stars and strays / Paul Thigpen.
    p. cm.
  Includes index.
  ISBN-13: 978-0-86716-724-5 (pbk. alk. paper)
  ISBN-10: 0-86716-724-6 (pbk. : alk. paper) 1. Christian life—Catholic authors. 2. Last words. 3. Christian life—Quotations, maxims, etc. 4. Catholics—Quotations, maxims, etc. 5. Jesus Christ—Words. I. Title.

BX2350.3.T485 2006
282.092—dc22
[B]

2006010492

ISBN-10: 0-86716-724-6
ISBN-13: 978-0-86716-724-5
Copyright ©2006 Paul Thigpen. All rights reserved.

Published by Servant Books, an imprint of St. Anthony Messenger Press
28 W. Liberty St.
Cincinnati, OH 45202
www.AmericanCatholic.org

Printed in the United States of America

Printed on acid-free paper

06 07 08 09 10 5 4 3 2 1

For my father, Travis T. Thigpen, Sr.,
who placed his hands on my head
and blessed me on his deathbed
like the patriarchs of old,
with last words that continue to inspire me
after many long years:
"May your ministry go out to
all the ends of the earth,
and may you reach up and touch
the face of God."

If I were a writer of books, I would compile a register, with a comment, of the various deaths of men. Whoever would teach people to die, would at the same time teach them to live.
—Michel de Montaigne (1533–1592), *Essaies,* vol. 3, ch. 19

CONTENTS

A Note About the Sources and Scope of This Book

Accounts of a person's final words and circumstances sometimes vary and can be difficult to confirm, since few die in public settings. Some popular stories, often retold, may even be apocryphal. Reports about the death of the influential French philosopher and mathematician René Descartes provide a case in point.

The narrative most often circulated has the Frenchman saying dramatically: "My soul, you have long been held captive; the hour has now come for you to quit your prison, to leave the trammels of this body. Suffer then this separation with joy and courage." Yet Descartes' valet insisted that the dying man was actually in a coma and expired without saying anything at all.

Nevertheless, even disputed accounts may contain within them a fine gem of wisdom. So some of them I have included in this collection without apology.

I should also note that the notion of "last words" is broadly understood here so as to secure the greatest opportunity for including quotations of interest. As in most such collections, I may present not only the very last sentence or two uttered by the dying but also significant remarks made in the final hours or even days before death, as well as an occasional excerpt from a last will or tomb-stone inscription.

Since comments over the course of hours (or even minutes) may range widely in subject matter, some of the individuals quoted may appear multiple times in this book across several categories. In this way each significant statement receives the particular attention it is due. The name index at the back of the book will allow the reader to identify and collect in one place, if desired, the various last words of a single dying person.

One last remark: Why are only Catholics included here? One obvious reason is that a general collection of last words would only duplicate the work of several other volumes already available. A more specific reason is that the intent of this book is spiritual. Rather than simply reciting last words, we seek—through categorization and commentary—to uncover particular theological and moral truths reflected in the statements. Especially with regard to subjects such as the last rites, the Eucharist, the communion of saints and apparitions, narrowing the book's scope to make it explicitly Catholic has allowed for a sharper focus.

ONE

"I Have Set You an Example"

WHAT CAN WE LEARN FROM LAST WORDS?

> *For I have set you an*
> *example, that you also*
> *should do as I have done.*
> —John 13:15

THE INFAMOUS MEXICAN REVOLUTIONARY PANCHO Villa was ambushed and assassinated on his ranch in Chihuahua in 1923. His reported last words? "Don't let it end like this. Tell them I said something."

If the report is true, Villa's dying statement points to the great significance we assign to a person's last words. Villa actually seemed embarrassed not to have ready some memorable line to pronounce before he left the stage for good. A farewell fabricated by those he left behind was preferable to an admission that his colorful life had ended in stammering or silence.

An avid concern with last words is deeply rooted in Western culture. So highly did the ancient Hebrews esteem the tradition of their early patriarchs' dying discourses that the words became part of their Scripture—and part of their shared self-identity. Jacob's blessing, for example, foretold the varied destinies of his twelve sons and the nation their descendants would form (see Genesis 49). The final statements of Moses (Deuteronomy 33),

Joshua (Joshua 24) and David (1 Kings 2) have their honored places in the Bible as well.

Our ancient classical heritage displayed a similar interest in dying declarations. The last words of the Greek philosopher Socrates, after he had drunk poisonous hemlock at the command of the Athenian authorities, were rather mundane: "I owe a cock to Asclepius; will you remember to pay the debt?" Yet the philosopher Plato dutifully recorded and publicized the words, suggesting that in the eyes of that admiring disciple, even so prosaic a remark was to be prized.

Farewell statements have always assumed a place of honor within the Christian tradition as well. The followers of Jesus took care to chronicle his last words. Christians went on to record last words of the saints, especially the martyrs.

After multiple millennia the tradition of cherished last words has become a cultural institution of sorts. As social and spiritual heirlooms, statements of the dying are gathered, treasured and handed down. In fact, so many collections of such materials have been published that "Last Words" is actually an official subject category in the United States Library of Congress classification system.

So why exactly are these words so important to us?

Prophetic Words

Though his own final lines were rather ordinary, Socrates once alluded to the ancient Greek belief that the words of the dying sometimes possess preternatural or prophetic powers. The Old Testament deathbed pronouncements already cited reflect a similar belief. Some of the quotes included in this collection grab our attention because they seem to confirm that those about to die occasionally display an uncanny ability to predict, or at least anticipate, the future.

One example is Lukas Etlin, the Swiss-American Benedictine brother who founded Caritas, a network of humanitarian organizations. He told some Catholic schoolgirls one morning that Christians must be ready to die and meet their Lord at any time, noting specifically that such an unexpected death could result from an auto collision. (This caught the girls' attention, because automobiles were not nearly as common in 1927 as they are now.) A few hours later Brother Lukas lay beside the highway, indeed dead from a traffic accident.

The young Spanish Carmelite known as Maria Teresa of Jesus Quevado provides a more explicitly prophetic example. Though she was only nineteen years old and seemed to be in good health, she predicted during Advent of 1949 that she would be in heaven with our Lady the following year, in time to celebrate the papal proclamation of the dogma of the Assumption. A few months later she died of tubercular meningitis.

In many similar cases the dying were no doubt such close friends of God that their last words came at the prompting of the Holy Spirit. Others, perhaps, standing at the threshold of another world, could simply peer into realms usually hidden from the rest of us. As the approach of death stripped away the immediate preoccupations and distractions of this life, the field of vision was uncluttered for the perception of more distant realities.

If that's in fact the case, it's not surprising that last words are sometimes associated with deathbed visions, voices and omens—similar to those reported in connection with near-death experiences. Saint Clare of Assisi said she saw Jesus enter the room as she lay dying. Saint Pio of Pietrelcina saw our Lord's mother as well as his own. Mary I, queen of England, beheld angels and heard them singing.

Words of Wisdom

Last words command our attention for other important reasons as well.

First, the clarity of vision sometimes brought on by death's approach encompasses not only the next world but also this one. As scenes of life on earth recede, the big picture emerges. In the brilliant light of eternity, the alluring beauty of all that must pass away soon fades.

The dying often find that they are beginning at last to see as God sees. In short, with death often comes wisdom. So dying words are precious because they may crystallize insights for the sake of those left behind.

Saint Gianna Beretta Molla, an Italian mother and medical doctor, put it this way on her deathbed: "If you only knew how differently things are judged at the hour of death, how vain certain things appear to which we give such importance in the world!"

Second, dying words carry a certain compelling authority because, as the old legal maxim goes, *Nemo moriturus praesumitur mentiri:* "No one dying is presumed to lie." Why not? The French dramatist Phillipe Quinault explained: "He who has only a moment to live has no longer anything to hide."

If we want to hear the truth, then—however startling, however uncomfortable it may be—we do well to stand listening beside the deathbed. Lope de Vega, the Spanish dramatist and poet, provides one humorous example of dying honesty. When told he was about to die, he allegedly remarked: "All right, then, I'll say it: Dante makes me sick."

Third, last words strike us as valuable because they are often so costly to the one who speaks them. Shakespeare's observation from *Richard II* comes to mind here: "O, but they say the tongues of dying men / Enforce attention like deep harmony. / Where words are scarce, they are seldom spent in vain, / For they breathe truth that breathe their words in pain" (II.1.5–8).

Think of Saint Chi Zhuze, a Chinese Catholic who was brutally tortured and executed for his faith. When the soldiers began the ordeal by cutting off his arm, he told them firmly: "Cut me in as many pieces as you wish and you will see that every piece is a Catholic!"

Finally, dying declarations may arrest our attention simply because of their finality. They are irrevocable; they cannot be taken back; they will stand, without revision, forever. The weight of such permanence may impress them indelibly on our hearts.

Consider, for example, the moving last words of Blessed Elizabeth of the Trinity, the French Carmelite and spiritual writer. A few days before her death at the end of a long illness, she declared: "Everything passes. In the evening of life, love alone remains."

The Culmination of a Life

In many cases dying words reflect the culmination of a life, the fruit of countless thoughts and actions, ripened at last on this day when God comes to harvest the soul. So we find them intriguing as a sort of motto for the life that is ending, a spoken epitaph engraved, if not on a tombstone, then at least on the minds of those listening.

Often final thoughts reveal a firm sense of vocation, religious or secular, the core of a self-identity that remains to the very end. Generals may speak of strategy, statesmen of politics, musicians of their compositions, bishops of their flocks. Conrad Hilton, founder of the famous hotel chain, gave final instructions to guests: "Leave the shower curtain on the *inside* of the tub."

For others, essential character is revealed, or a particular virtue is crystallized. The humility of Saint Francis of Assisi, for example, was perfectly captured in his request to be laid out to die naked on the ground. And how else could Saint John the Almsgiver breathe his last except with instructions to give his very last penny to the poor? Other sources say he even gave away the sheet covering him on his deathbed.

Of course, the character revealed is not always lovely. Dying words of rulers may display their will to power; of scholars, their arrogance; of skeptics, their defiance of heaven; of wastrels, their self-indulgence. Some last words are suicide notes revealing the depths of despair.

Yet even in these cases, the words of the dying have much to teach us. These last moments provide tragic object lessons, vividly portraying a fate we must by all means flee. The chilling scenes of impenitence and hope-lessness, or decay and dissolution, can awaken us to repen-tance—and prayer for God's mercy on the departed souls and on our own.

Death at the Heart of the Gospel

For Christians all these reasons for meditating on last words become even more deeply compelling. Dying moments present us with much more than helpful epi-grams, telling vignettes or morality tales. If we're willing to reflect on them carefully, they can actually point us to fundamental realities—to the very heart of God.

At the center of the gospel, after all, stands a cross on which hangs a dying Man, crying out his last words. Through his sacrificial death, the redemption of a broken world becomes possible. The Son of God joins to himself our very nature, offers it up to his Father, restores and remakes it in his own image. In that final moment his cross becomes a new Tree of Life, his anguished cries become its fruits, and he offers them for our nourishment and healing.

Why does such life flow from death? Because the cross gives way to the empty tomb, from whose depths the life springs. Only in Jesus' resurrection is the meaning of his death fully revealed. His conquest of the grave transforms his suffering and sacrifice into a mighty river that flows from this world into the next, where the fleeting life of earth converges at last with the eternal life of heaven.

All Catholics have received in the grace of baptism an initial share of this eternal life. Yet we must never forget that "all of us who have been baptized into Christ Jesus were baptized into his death" as well (Romans 6:3). Only "if we have been united with him in a death like his" will we "be united with him in a resurrection like his" (v. 5).

In this as in all things, we must imitate our Lord. First the cross, then the empty tomb. First the agony, then the glory.

Meanwhile, we must not fail to recognize the dark possibility lurking here: because of the great and terrible gift of human free will, death may in some cases lead not to everlasting glory but to endless woe. Admittedly, we are peering here into a mystery, and we must leave in God's hands the final judgment of every soul. But Saint Augustine's observation is well taken: based on their last words, we might well conclude that the two thieves cruci-fied on either side of Jesus chose opposite destinies. Their examples warn us against presumption as well as despair.

The death of each Catholic, then, takes on a critical significance for those of us left behind. Whichever partic-ular "cross" may be the occasion for that death—sickness, accidental injury, malice of enemies, old age—it represents a splinter of Christ's own cross. So the final utterance may well be, in one way or another, some echo of Christ's own last words. We would do well to listen carefully.

Our Lord's Example

Since faithful Catholics have always sought to imitate their Lord in death as in life, their parting statements and circumstances seem to fall rather naturally into categories drawn from the last words of his final days. Even in cases where the dying are known to have wandered far away from Christ's teaching and example, they often unintentionally fulfill some prophecy or illustrate some warning that our Lord issued in his last hours.

In this collection, then, the last words of Christ will serve as a way of organizing and illuminating the last words of those who have borne his name as Christians. If we consider not simply the final sentences he spoke before dying but also noteworthy statements from Jesus' final days, then his recorded last words are rather extensive. From our Lord's last twenty-four hours we have numerous farewell instructions to the apostles, solemn pronouncements at the Last Supper, prayers in Gethsemane and brief but poignant exchanges with the authorities who brought about his execution. When we add Christ's teachings from the last seven days before his crucifixion, we find that the Gospels provide for our reflection a remarkable treasury of Jesus' final thoughts.

Given the reality that all who have received baptism have received through that sacrament a share in Christ's life, there were only two criteria for choosing the people quoted in this collection: they were baptized in the Catholic church, and we can profit from what they said at the end of life. So readers will find here, as the book's subtitle suggests, both great saints and great sinners, famous stars and infamous strays. From each of them, whatever their final condition, we have something important to learn about our Lord, about ourselves and about this inescapable mystery we call death.

TWO

"For This I Was Born"
VOCATION

> *For this I was born, and*
> *for this I came into the*
> *world, to testify to the*
> *truth.*
> —John 18:37

A POPULAR IRISH PIANIST OF THE NINETEENTH CENTURY, so the oft-told story goes, lay dying far from home in another country. Those who were with him concluded that it was time to call in a clergyman, but they weren't sure of his religious affiliation. So they asked him: "Are you a Catholic or a Calvinist?"

His answer—and his final declaration before he died—was firm: "I am a pianist."

Perhaps the feisty Irishman was simply weary of the religious divisions that had plagued his native land for centuries. Perhaps his devotion to his career was so passionate that it had in fact become for him a religion. In either case, his remark calls to mind the references to personal vocation so common among those facing death.

Throughout the last week of his life, Jesus himself made such references. Praying in the Garden of Gethsemane, he declared that he had accomplished the work his Father had given him to do (see John 17:4). On trial before Pilate, he spoke of his reason for being born: "to testify to the truth."

Echoing his Lord, the apostle Paul wrote to friends about his lifework not long before his death: "The time of my departure has come. I have fought the good fight, I have finished the race, I have kept the faith" (2 Timothy 4:6–7).

In their final hours many Catholics have demonstrated much the same kind of focus on their personal vocation, whether religious or secular. What has occupied their thoughts for a lifetime not surprisingly occupies their thoughts at death.

As with Saint Paul, in the last words of some we detect a strong sense of accomplishment and closure. The task has been long and demanding, but it is now done. So Saint Francis of Assisi said to his friars: "I have done what is mine to do; may Christ teach you what is yours."

Others, however, express a wistful, sometimes bittersweet desire to keep living just a little longer for the sake of work still incomplete. Belgian composer Guillame Lekeu cried out as he died of typhoid: "So many works unfinished! My quartet!"

Football coach Vince Lombardi told his priest: "I'm not afraid to die. I'm not afraid to meet my God now. But what I do regret is that there is so damned much left to be done on earth!" Such comments display a poignant loyalty to a life mission.

A few of the dying even hope their vocation will somehow extend beyond death. The dying wish of French landscape painter Jean-Baptiste-Camille Corot was, "I hope with all my heart there will be painting in heaven." The warrior King Edward I of England told his soldiers as he died in battle: "Wrap my bones in a hammock and have them carried before the army, so that I may still lead the way to victory."

The last words in all these scenes spur us to give ourselves passionately and faithfully to the task before us. In that way we too can pray to our heavenly Father at the end of life, as Jesus did, "I glorified you on earth by finishing the work that you gave me to do" (John 17:4).

* * *

Saint Thomas Aquinas (c. 1225–1274), the Italian Dominican philosopher, theologian and doctor of the church, addressed the Eucharist he received on his deathbed:

> I receive you, the price of my redemption. I receive you, Companion of my life on this earth. All my studies, all my vigils, and all my labors have been for love of you. I have preached you and taught you. Never have I said anything against you. If anything was not well said, that is to be attributed to my ignorance….I submit all to the judgment and correction of the Holy Roman Church, in whose obedience I now leave this world.

Robert Bruce, king of Scotland (1274–1329), had vowed to go on a Crusade in the Holy Land but died before he could go. He gave these last instructions:

> I will that as soon as I shall be dead, you take my heart from my body, and have it well embalmed. You will also

take as much money from my treasury as shall appear to you sufficient to perform your journey, as well as for all those whom you may choose to take with you in your train. You will then deposit your charge at the Holy Sepulchre where our Lord was buried.

You will not be sparing of expense, but will provide yourself with such company and such things as may be suitable to your rank. And wherever you pass, you will let it be known that you bear the heart of King Robert of Scotland, which you are carrying beyond the seas by his command, since his body cannot go there....

I shall now die in peace, since I know that the most valiant and accomplished knight of my kingdom will perform that for me which I am unable to do for myself.

Blessed Pope John XXIII (1881–1963), who summoned the Second Vatican Council, spoke to his family members gathered around his deathbed: "Do you remember how I never thought of anything else in life but being a priest?"

Nicolas Boileau (1636–1711) was a French poet and literary critic. He took great satisfaction in noting as he died: "It is a great consolation to a dying poet to have never written anything against morality."

Terence J. Cooke (1921–1983), cardinal archbishop of New York, led the United States Bishops Pro-Life Campaign and considered his work an "apostolate on behalf of life." He wrote a farewell letter to his flock, which was read in Masses on Pro-Life Sunday, October 9,

1983, three days after his death from cancer:

> The "gift of life," God's special gift, is no less beautiful when it is accompanied by illness or weakness, hunger or poverty, mental or physical handicaps, loneliness or old age. Indeed, at these times, human life gains extra splendor as it requires our special care, concern and reverence. It is in and through the weakest of human vessels that the Lord continues to reveal the power of his love. ... At this grace-filled time of my life, as I experience suffering in union with Jesus Our Lord and Redeemer, I offer gratitude to Almighty God for giving me the opportunity to continue my apostolate on behalf of life.

Saint Thérèse of the Child Jesus (Lisieux) (1873–1897), the French Carmelite nun and doctor of the church, had always prayed that she could join Christ in his sufferings, seeing this as part of her vocation. She said: "All I wrote about my desires for suffering, oh, it's true just the same! And I am not sorry for delivering myself up to love. Oh, no, I'm not sorry. On the contrary.... Never would I have believed it was possible to suffer so much, never, never! I cannot explain this except by the ardent desire I have had to save souls."

Dominique Bouhours (1628–1702) was a French grammarian. Unable to resist providing one last instruction about propriety in language, he offered two alternative forms of his dying declaration: "I am about to—or I am going to—die: either expression is used."

Jacques-Louis David (1748–1825) was a French painter who dropped dead as he was indicating corrections to be made on a copy of his painting *Leonidas at Thermopylae:* "Too dark... too light....The dimming of the light is not well enough indicated....This place is blurred....However, I must admit, that's a unique head of Leonidas."

Eugène Delacroix (1799–1863) was a French Romantic painter. He said brightly just before he died: "Oh, if I get well, I will do wonderful things! My mind is bubbling with ideas!"

Armand-Jean Plessis, Duc de Richelieu (1582–1642), the famous French cardinal and statesman, was at one time the virtual dictator of his country. So fully did he identify himself with his political career rather than his clerical responsibilities that when he was asked by the attending priest beside his deathbed, "Do you pardon all your enemies?" he replied: "I have none save those of the state."

Miguel de Cervantes (1547–1616), the Spanish novelist best known for his *Don Quixote de la Mancha,* wrote in a last letter to the king: "Time is short, agony grows, hope lessens. Only the will to live keeps me alive. Would that life might last until I might kiss the feet of your Excellency!... But if it be decreed that I must die, Heaven's will be done! May your Excellency know, at least, what my wish was, and know also that he had in me a servant so faithful as to wish to have served your Excellency even after death!"

Sophie Charlotte, Duchesse d'Alençon (1847–1897), Bavarian-born but transplanted to France, was a celebrated philanthropist who dedicated her life to charitable efforts. As she presided one evening over a charity bazaar in Paris, the room caught fire, causing panic-stricken guests to trample one another in their attempt to flee the building. Workers from a nearby site raced into the blaze to rescue the injured women and children.

They found the duchess calmly sitting in her booth. "Because of my title, I was the first to enter here," she declared. "I shall be the last to go out." She died along with more than 120 other victims.

Umberto II (1904–1982), Italy's last king, reigned only a month before the people voted to abolish the monarchy. Dying in exile, his last word was simply *"Italia!"*

Pablo Picasso (1881–1973), the controversial Spanish painter who was a founder of the Cubist school, seemed uncertain at the end about his accomplishments—indeed, about the artistic endeavor altogether. He concluded on his deathbed: "Painting remains to be invented."

Richard III (1452–1485), king of England, had to fight rebel forces seeking to overthrow him. In the Battle of Bosworth Field, his horse was killed, and his comrades urged him to withdraw. But he shouted: "I will die king of England! I will not budge a foot!" Walking into the thick of the battle, fighting fiercely, he was quickly felled.

Thomas Fantet de Lagny (1660–1734) was a French mathematician. When almost entirely unconscious, he was asked, "What is the square of twelve?" He answered quickly: "One hundred and forty-four."

Patrick Sarsfield, Earl of Lucan (1650–1693), was an Irish soldier. Ever devoted to his homeland, when he was mortally wounded on the battlefield in the service of the French, he put his hand to his wound, drew it forth covered with blood and said: "Would to God this were shed for Ireland!"

Honoré de Balzac (1799–1850) was a French writer. As he lay dying after years of poor health, he spoke of one of his fictional characters, a physician who worked scientific miracles: "Only Bianchon can save me."

Pierre Du Terrail, Seigneur de Bayard (c. 1473–1524), was a heroic French soldier called "The Knight without Fear and above Reproach." Mortally wounded while fighting in Italy, he encouraged his comrades: "Weep not, for I die in the bed of honor. I have lived long enough. The only thing that distresses me is that I can no longer serve my prince."

Charles Chavez (d. 1910) was a Peruvian aviator whose plane crashed during a flying competition. For several days he lay semiconscious and delirious, repeating these last words: "Higher! Always higher!"

François-René, Vicomte de Chateaubriand (1768–1848), was a French author and statesman of revolutionary sympathies. He died of natural causes during the revolution that set up a republican government. When told that there was fighting in the street, he exclaimed: "I want to go there!"

Désiré-Félicien-François-Joseph Mercier (1851–1926) was cardinal archbishop of Malines, Belgium. Just before he received the last rites, he prayed: "I thirst to lead souls to you, O Lord!"

Louis-Joseph, Marquis de Montcalm (1712–1759), was a French military leader. He was mortally wounded in the Battle of Quebec, which led to the loss of New France to England. Dying the next day, he said: "Praise God that I will not live to see the surrender of Quebec!"

Manuel Luis Quezon (1878–1944) was the first president of the Philippines. He died of tuberculosis in Washington, D.C., as he listened to a radio broadcast reporting that American forces had landed in New Guinea and were poised to liberate his homeland. His last words were full of hope: "Just six hundred miles!"

Marie-Thérèse-Luise de Savoie-Carignan Lamballe (1749–1792) was superintendent of the household of Marie Antoinette, queen of France. Ordered by the French revolutionaries to swear an oath of allegiance to liberty and equality and to renounce her loyalty to the king and queen, she agreed to all but denouncing her sovereigns. As she was dragged out to be hacked into pieces, she shouted defiantly: "Fie on the horror!"

Paul Scarron (1610–1660) was a French dramatist and poet known for his comedy. He said to his weeping family: "Ah, my children, you cannot cry for me as much as I have made you laugh!"

Samuel Alphonsus Stritch (1887–1958), cardinal archbishop of Chicago, was appointed head of the Congregation for the Propagation of the Faith in Rome. Celebrating Mass for the first time after having an arm amputated, he said: "Well, I feel like a priest again." Soon afterward he suffered a stroke and died.

Arturo Toscanini (1867–1957), the Italian-American orchestra conductor, suffered several strokes. A few days before he died, he imagined that he was conducting a rehearsal: "No, not like that, more smoothly, please, more smoothly. Let's repeat. More smoothly. That's it, good, now it's right."

Sir Everard Digby (1578–1606) was an English Catholic convert who was hung, drawn and quartered for his part in a plot to blow up Parliament and overthrow King James I, who persecuted Catholics. When the executioner cut out his heart and shouted, "Here is the heart of a traitor!" he retorted: "Thou liest!"

Anne-Robert-Jacques Turgot (1727–1781) was the French minister of finance. Scolded for ruining his health by working too much, he replied: "You blame me for attempting too much, but you know that in my family, we die of gout at fifty."

Claude-Louis-Hector, Duke of Villars (1653–1734), was marshal of France and one of the greatest generals in French history. As he lay dying a natural death in his old age, someone noted that an English commander had recently died in battle. He said, with apparent envy: "I had always contended that that man was born luckier than I."

James (Jimmy) John Walker (1881–1946) was an Irish-American mayor of New York City and a prominent leader of the Democratic Party. When his nurse ordered him to get in bed, he complained: "Am I not the master of my own house?"

She responded: "Yes, Mr. Walker, but..."

The old politician interrupted her: "Oh, you must be a good Democrat."

When she admitted that she was, he said: "In that case I shall abide by the wishes of a fair constituent."

He returned to bed and promptly died.

Blessed Helen de Chappotin (1839–1904), known as Mary of the Passion, was founder of the Franciscan Missionaries of Mary. Not long before she died, she told the sisters of her order: "When I die, my death will leave a great void for the institute. However, you must not be afraid; the institute will follow its path just the same. If it were my work it would perish with me, but it is God's work, and it will live."

Saint Anselm (1033–1109) was an Italian philosopher, theologian and monk who became archbishop of Canterbury, England. As he died, he said with resignation: "Yes, if it be his will, I shall obey it willingly. But were he to let me stay with you a little longer till I had resolved a problem about the origin of the soul, I would gladly accept the boon; for I do not know whether anyone will work it out when I am gone."

Rudy Vallée (1901–1986), the American singer and entertainer, was viewing a TV broadcast of ceremonies commemorating the centennial of the Statue of Liberty when he said to his wife: "I wish we could be there. You know how I love a party." Then he took a breath and died.

Maurice Chevalier (1888–1972), the charming French entertainer, died recalling the title of a stage song: *"Y'a d'la Joie!"* ("There's fun in the air!").

Antoine Carème (1784–1833) was a French master chef who was tasting food in his kitchen when he died suddenly. His last words: "The quenelles are good, only they were prepared too hastily. You must shake the saucepan lightly."

Saint Hilary (c. 315–368), bishop of Poitiers in what is now France, was an influential theologian and a doctor of the church. After many long years of battling the Arian heresy and even suffering exile for opposing the Arian emperor, he summoned his courage at the hour of death by recalling his years of heroic ministry: "Soul, you have served Christ these seventy years, and are you afraid to die? Go out, soul, go out!"

Pierre-Auguste Renoir (1841–1919), the French Impressionist painter, showed that a great artist is always trying to grow professionally. His last words: "Today I learned something!"

Turlough O'Carolan (1670–1738) was an itinerant Irish bard, blinded by smallpox, who repaid his banqueting hosts' hospitality with the songs he composed, to harp accompaniment. At the end he called for a cup of his beloved *usquebaugh* (Irish whiskey), observing: "It would be hard if two such friends should part at least without kissing."

Jean-Baptiste Lully (1632–1687) was a French composer who died of gangrene, probably caused by an accidental blow of the heavy stick with which he kept the tempo while conducting. The attending priest told him that his illness was divine punishment for composing music for the theater, and he withheld absolution until Lully had an opera score, which was lying beside the bed, burned on the spot.

After his confessor left, a friend lamented the lost score. But the composer replied calmly: "That's nothing to worry about. You see, I had another copy in my desk."

Saint Louis Orione (1872–1940) was the Italian founder of the Hermits of Divine Providence. A nurse scolded him for having worked too hard when she learned that he had just written twenty-two letters to be mailed. He replied: "It's all right. We'll have a long rest in Paradise."

Stephen Eckert (1869–1923) was a Canadian Capuchin priest who tirelessly served the African-American community, especially the poor, in Milwaukee. Dying of pneumonia at age fifty-three, he lamented: "Here I lie idle, while thousands of souls are perishing!"

THREE

"Your Will Be Done"
A CCEPTANCE

> *Again he went away for*
> *the second time and*
> *prayed, "My Father, if*
> *this cannot pass unless I*
> *drink it, your will be*
> *done."*
> —Matthew 26:42

SOCIOLOGISTS WHO STUDY THE EXPERIENCES OF THE dying speak of our response to death in terms of stages. Those with the luxury of knowing ahead of time that death is approaching will typically move through denial and anger, bargaining and depression. But if they hope to find peace at the end of life, they must sooner or later reach the final stage of grief: the place of acceptance.

Jesus spoke often of his mission in this world, predicting that he would suffer and die at the hand of his enemies (see Luke 9:22, 44; 18:31–33). He clearly accepted this destiny, knowing that it was his Father's will and the path for the world's salvation (Matthew 20:28). He even refused to flee from the ordeal when the opportunity to do so presented itself (Luke 13:31–33).

Nevertheless, in those terrible moments in Gethsemane just hours before his crucifixion, our Lord struggled. Though fully God, he was also fully human, and his human nature felt horror and revulsion at the prospect of events to come. He never sinned by opposing his Father's will. But in his cries of grief we hear the last words of a man engaged in one final, awful battle to accept and embrace death.

Jesus won the fight, though the victory left him bleeding before his foes ever laid a hand on him (see Luke 22:44). In the end he was able to echo his mother's *fiat,* her yes to God, given many years before at the moment of his conception. Just as her words of acceptance had allowed his mission to begin, his words of acceptance now allowed the mission to be completed: "Your will be done" (Matthew 26:42).

In the last words of many Catholics, especially the saints, we meet a similar shouldering of the burden of God's will—not just death but the anguish that might precede it, both physical and mental. Unlike their Lord, who knew no sin, they long for the purging of their souls to be complete. So they accept the suffering as a form of penance, a scouring brush in the hand of God.

At times the dying remarks seem almost effortless, and we may wonder whether we could ever meet death with such calm fortitude. Nevertheless, we should keep in mind that, in many cases, the struggles that led to acceptance are hidden from our view. We're listening to the last moments in their Gethsemane, not the first.

The phrase "resignation to the will of God," so often used in older spiritual texts to describe the deaths of saints, may be misleading today. The nuances of the term *resignation* have shifted to convey something quite passive, even indifferent, rather than active and hopeful. And we do encounter in some of these final words what seems little more than a sigh and a shrug, such as British biographer and publisher Maisie Ward's comment a few days before she died at the age of eighty-six: "I still have enthusiasm. But what use is enthusiasm without energy?"

Other last words reflect a contentment apparently more casual than spiritual. As Empress Maria Theresa of Austria lay dying, one of her children asked whether she was comfortable. She answered: "No, but comfortable enough to die."

Yet most of the last words here suggest an eagerness to leave this world, if the departure would be pleasing to the Lord. Hungering to do God's will, these men and women run out to embrace "Sister Death," as Saint Francis called her, smiling as they go. Their fervor displays a passion not for her but rather for the One who waits for them at her side. For "the Lord's will," as the dying biblical scholar Cyril Martindale put it, "is the most lovable of all."

* * *

Saint Jean Baptiste de la Salle (1651–1719) was asked at the end whether he accepted with joy his sufferings. He replied: "Yes. I adore in all things the designs of God in my regard."

Chiara Luce Badano (1971–1990) was a young Italian cancer victim. Not long before her death she wrote to Chiara Lubich, the founder of the Focolare movement:

> Medicine has quit the fight. Only God can do something now. Stopping the therapy means that the pain has increased in my back, and I can hardly turn on my side anymore. Will I manage to be faithful to Jesus forsaken? I feel so small, and the road ahead seems so steep. I some-times feel suffocated by the pain. But it's my spouse who is coming to me, isn't it? I too want to repeat with you, "If you want it, Jesus, I want it too."

Blessed Damien de Veuster (1840–1889) was a Belgian-born missionary priest of the Fathers of the Sacred Hearts of Jesus and Mary. At his request he was sent to evangelize the people of Hawaii and then to serve the leper colony on the island of Molakai. Dying of lep-rosy contracted through his work, he concluded: "Well! God's will be done! He knows best. My work, with all its faults and failures, is in his hands, and before Easter I shall see my Savior."

Saint Vincent de Paul (c. 1580–1660) was a French priest and founder of the Congregation of the Mission, which served orphans, the sick and the poor and which ransomed slaves. He said a few days before he died, as he was going to sleep: "It is Brother Sleep. Soon the sister, Death, will come."

Louis XIII (1601–1643), king of France, said after learning that he had only two hours to live: "Well, my God, I consent with all my heart."

Saint Bernard of Clairveaux (1090–1153), French Cistercian abbot, mystic, spiritual writer and doctor of the church, said at the very end: "May God's will be done."

Pope Saint Pius X (1835–1914), after receiving the Eucharist and with both hands on a crucifix, came to the end of his life with the words "I resign myself completely."

Anne of Austria (1601–1666), queen of France, was the wife of Louis XIII. Noting, "It is time to depart," she said to a friend who was weeping at the foot of her deathbed: "Consider what I owe to God, the favor he has shown me, and the great indulgence for which I am beholden to him."

Pope Saint Pius V (1504–1572) instituted moral and ecclesiastical reforms, formed a Christian alliance against the Turks and revised the breviary and missal. He prayed on his deathbed: "Lord, increase my pain, but may it please you also to increase my patience!"

Lucrezia Borgia (1480–1519), the Italian Duchess of Ferrara who devoted the end of her rather colorful life to charity and education, wrote in a letter to Pope Leo X:

> Having suffered for more than two months, early in the morning on the fourteenth of the present, as it pleased God, I gave birth to a daughter, and hoped then to find relief from my sufferings, but I did not, and shall be compelled to pay my debt to nature. So great is the favor which our merciful Creator has shown me, that I approach the end of my life with pleasure, knowing that in a few hours, after receiving for the last time all the holy sacraments of the Church, I shall be released.

Charles V (1500–1558), Holy Roman Emperor, retired to a monastery, where he died two years after his abdication. Gazing at a silver crucifix and sighing, he whispered: "It is time.... Ay, Jesus!"

Louis XIV (1638–1715), king of France, was known as the "Sun King." He said to two valets around his deathbed: "Why do you weep? Did you think I was immortal?"

Saint John Bosco (1815–1888), Italian priest and founder of the Salesian Fathers, departed this life with the phrase from Gethsemane: "Your will be done."

Frédéric Chopin (1810–1849), the French-Polish pianist and composer, died of tuberculosis. On his deathbed he said to his sister: "I love God and man. I am happy so to die. Do not weep, my sister."

Later he said to his doctors: "Perhaps you have erred about my sickness. But God does not err. He punishes me, and I bless him for it. Oh, how good is God to punish me here below! Oh, how good God is!"

Gary Cooper (1901–1961), the American actor, said as he lay dying of cancer: "It is God's will."

Saint Frances of Rome (1384–1440), the Italian mystic and visionary who established a community of Benedictine nuns, murmured: "The angel has finished his task. He beckons me to follow him."

Saint Joseph of Cupertino (1603–1663) was an Italian Franciscan friar and mystic. His last words were a paean of praise: "Praised be God! Blessed be God! May the holy will of God be done!"

Alfred Thayer Mahan (1840–1914) was an American naval officer and historian. While gazing at a tree outside his hospital window, he said to a nurse: "If a few more quiet years were granted me, I might see and enjoy these things. But God is just, and I am content."

Lorenzo de' Medici (1449–1492), also known as "Lorenzo the Magnificent," was a Florentine political and cultural leader. After suffering from a wasting illness, he was informed by his sister that his medical prognosis was hopeless. He answered: "If it is God's will, nothing can be more pleasant to me than death." His lips moved as a passage from Scripture was read aloud to him. A silver crucifix was placed against his lips; he kissed it and expired.

Pope Pius XI (1857–1939) denounced Hitler's Nazism, Mussolini's anti-Semitism and Communism; supported overseas missions; and advocated measures for world peace. Dying of a heart condition, he ended with the words: "My soul is in the hands of God."

Francisco Suárez (1548–1617) was a Spanish Jesuit spiritual writer. He observed: "I would never have believed it so sweet to die."

Blessed Helen de Chappotin (Mary of the Passion), dying of a septic abscess on her leg, received her last Holy Communion and then asked not to be disturbed: "Don't concern yourselves; leave me alone with God. Very soon, I shall be very well indeed."

Venerable Solanus Casey (1870–1957) was an American Capuchin priest known for his miracle working and wise spiritual direction. The nurse at his deathbed regretted that so many intravenous feedings had left his hands raw and red. "Well, Sister," he said, "don't feel badly about it. Look at our Lord's hands."

Venerable Genoveffa De Trois (1887–1949) was an Italian Franciscan tertiary whose lifelong illness she decided to offer to God as a sacrifice for others. In a letter written not long before she died, she mentioned what is regarded as her life motto: "I pray and I suffer; I suffer and I offer."

Saint Teresa Benedicta of the Cross (1891–1942), better known as Edith Stein, was a German Jewish philosopher, convert and Carmelite nun. Sent by the Nazis to the death camp at Auschwitz, not long before she was killed she was able to send a brief note to her sisters in the convent. It read in part: "I am content about everything. ... *Ave crux, spes unica.* [Hail to the cross, our only hope.]"

Marica Stankovik (1900–1957) was the Croatian founder of the lay community Associates of Christ the King. Imprisoned for her faith, she made her last words a prayer: "Your grace will do."

Jean Racine (1639–1699), the French dramatist, said at the end of a long, debilitating sickness: "I never had the strength to do penance. What a blessing for me that God has done me the mercy of sending me this penance."

Louis XVIII (1755–1824), king of France, lay dying from diabetes. As he awoke to hear the priest saying the last rites, he said to him: "Continue, since you have thought it necessary to begin. I am not afraid of death. It is only a bad king who does not know how to die."

Joyce Kilmer (1886–1918) was the American journalist and religious poet best known for the popular verse that begins: "I think that I shall never see / a poem lovely as a tree." Not long before he died fighting in the Second Battle of the Marne in France during World War I, he wrote a poem entitled "Prayer of a Soldier in France," which ended: "Lord, Thou didst suffer more for me / Than all the hosts of land and sea. / So let me render back again / This millionth of Thy gift. Amen."

Maggie Sinclair (1900–1925) was a Scottish Poor Clare who died of tuberculosis of the throat. While gasping for breath on her deathbed, she accidentally swallowed a wasp, which stung her already tormented throat. When asked whether she was all right, she replied through tears: "It is just another wee splinter of the cross."

FOUR

"It Is Finished"

Detachment

> *He said, "It is finished."*
> *Then he bowed his head*
> *and gave up his spirit.*
> —John 19:30

In the Twenty-third Psalm, that most familiar of prayers, King David reminds us that death casts a shadow across our lives (see v. 4). Those who live in fear of that darkness, the writer of Hebrews explains, are "held in slavery" (Hebrews 2:15). Whenever they must choose between what's right but risky on the one hand and what's wrong but safe on the other, they feel compelled to choose the latter. The drive for self-preservation makes a harsh taskmaster.

Must we fear the shadow? Or is it possible that, once we've accepted the reality of death, we can turn its shadow to our advantage? After all, having spent his youth as a shepherd, David knew well that such darkness can also serve as shade, a shield from blinding light and oppressive heat.

Like dazzling mirages, the fleeting glories of this world can deceive us. Power, possessions, prestige, popularity—their seductive brilliance is only borrowed, and it fades with the setting of the sun. The shadow of death, when it falls across our field of vision, can dim their luster.

Like blazing sands all around us, the wide expanse of life's demanding journey can tempt us to despair. Just when it seems we're overwhelmed, the shadow of death can grant relief: a reminder that the pain is not forever, that our task will one day be done. In the end, God willing, we'll find our rest and "dwell in the house of the Lord" forever (Psalm 23:6).

While fear of death's shadow leads to slavery, then, refreshment in that same shade can lead to freedom. It liberates us from the countless little chains that would bind us daily—the excessive love of wealth, status and all the rest. It also provides a season of comfort, a welcome release from the heavy burdens of the day.

The words of the dying can serve as a form of death's shadow, a source of correction and consolation. They warn us that this world is passing, that only God remains forever. They urge us to love him above all his creatures, to "have no other gods before" him (Exodus 20:3), because he alone is worthy to be served with all that we are (see Luke 10:27). We find solace at the sight of men and women casting their weariness aside to find peace at last.

This spiritual discipline of letting go and laying down is known in traditional devotional language as *detachment*. Some of the people quoted here practiced the discipline for many years before they died; their deaths simply brought the process to maturity. Others had ignored death's shadow; only when death stared them in the face were they provoked at last to disconnect.

In either case, at the moment of death they expressed profoundly the reality at the heart of Jesus' dying cry, anguished yet triumphant: "It is finished!" He had always loved his Father more than life itself; he never had been seduced or deceived by petty little idols masquerading as gods. Even so, in that moment, Jesus too had to let go of all things on this earth, even the good things: his mother's smile, the morning light, the laughter of children.

As he did, the weight of the whole world rolled off his bloody shoulders. His mission, his passion, was complete.

* * *

Pope Innocent XIII (1655–1724), when urged on his deathbed to create more cardinals, replied: "I am no longer of this world."

Pierre Toussaint (1766–1853) was a Haitian-American philanthropist. As he was dying he said to a friend: "God is with me." When asked whether he wanted anything, he answered: "Nothing on earth."

Marquis Louis-Joseph de Montcalm was commander of the French troops in North America. Mortally wounded on the battlefield, he concluded: "I have no more orders to give. I am busy with more important affairs, and the time which remains to me is short.... I die content."

Miguel de Cervantes, unable to speak at the end, wrote: "Goodbye, all that is charming. Goodbye, wit and gaiety. Goodbye, merry friends, for I am dying and wish to see you contented in another life."

Pope Innocent XI (1611–1689), when promised that his relatives would be cared for after he died, replied: "I have no house or family! God gave me the pontifical dignity, not for the advantage of my relatives, but for the good of the church and nations."

Peter (1392–1449), prince of Portugal, was the brother of Prince Henry the Navigator. He said as he lay dying: "O body of mine! I feel that you can do no more; and you, my spirit, why should you tarry here?"

Ludovico Ariosto (1474–1533), the Italian poet known for his epic *Orlando Furioso,* concluded at the end: "This is not my home."

Pope Leo XI (1535–1605) died of a fever less than a month after his election. When asked to name one of his nephews a cardinal, he told his assembled family: "Do not suggest to me any care for earthly concerns. You must speak to me now only about eternal matters."

Abba Saint Agatho (fourth century), one of the ancient desert fathers who mentored numerous monks, was pressed by the brothers to talk to them on his deathbed. He answered a few questions but ended: "Show me your charity by not speaking to me further, for I am busy."

Saint Monica (c. 330–387), a matron of North Africa, followed her son, Saint Augustine, to Italy. Though she had feared dying far away from home, she said on her deathbed: "Nothing is far from God, and I have no fear that he will not know at the end of the world from what place he is to raise me up."

Henry VII (1457–1509), king of England, insisted in his last will that his funeral should have respect for "the laud and praising of God, the health of our soul, and somewhat to our dignity royal, but avoiding damnable pomp and outrageous superfluities."

Saint Martin (c. 315–397) was bishop of Tours and a missionary to Gaul. As he lay on his deathbed, flat on his back and praying ceaselessly, a priest friend begged him to turn on his side so he could rest better. Martin replied: "Let me look toward heaven rather than earth, so I can set my soul now on the way that will bring it to the Lord."

Saint Camillus de Lellis (1550–1614) was an Italian priest and founder of the Order of the Ministers of the Sick (the Camellians). Two days before he died, he dictated a "last will and testament" to his confessor, which he had signed by seven priests and tied to his right arm to be buried with him. In it he let go of all he "possessed":

> To the devil I bequeath my sins against God.... To the world I bequeath all vanities, transitory things, worldly satisfactions, empty hopes, curiosities, even friends and relatives, so I may exchange what is passing for what is eternal, and all worldly curiosity for the true vision of the face of God.

Venerable John Henry Newman (1801–1890) was an English convert, cardinal and theologian. Not long before he died, he said: "I am not capable of doing anything more. I am not wanted. Now, mind what I say: it is not kind to me to wish to keep me longer from God."

Saint Francis Borgia (1510–1572) was a Spanish courtier who became father general of the Jesuits. When asked on his deathbed whether he wanted anything, he answered: "I want nothing but Jesus."

Antoine de Rivarol (1753–1801), a French author, said: "My friends, the great darkness is now approaching. These roses will change into poppies. It is time to contemplate eternity."

Álvaro de Luna (c. 1390–1453) was a Spanish politician who was ultimately executed by his political enemies. Informed that the post and hook he saw would soon have his head attached, he remarked: "It does not matter what they do with my body and head after my death."

Friedrich Leopold, Count von Stolberg-Stolberg (1750–1819) was a German romantic lyric poet. He asked his physician: "Tell me, will it truly be all over tomorrow or the next day?" The doctor said it would. He responded: "Praise God! Thanks! Thanks! I thank you with all my heart! Jesus Christ be praised!"

Pope Saint Pius X was deeply interested in social issues, especially the plight of the poor. His last will and testament declared: "I was born poor, I have lived poor, and I wish to die poor."

Saint Pio of Pietrelcina (1887–1968), popularly known as Padre Pio, was an Italian Capuchin priest famed as a miracle-worker. On the fiftieth anniversary of his receiving the stigmata, a few days before he died, a friend wished him another fifty years. Pio replied: "What harm have I ever done *you?*" The day before he died, he said to a fellow priest: "I belong more to the other world than to this one. Pray to our Lord that I might die."

Charles V (1337–1380), king of France, was a noted scholar and administrator known as "Charles the Wise." His last words: "Withdraw, my friends, withdraw and go away a little, so I can rest from the bother and labor I did not shirk."

Pope Clement XIV (1705–1774) on his deathbed was pressed to name some more cardinals. He refused: "I cannot and I will not do it. The Lord will judge my reasons." When the cardinals knelt and repeated their request, the dying man answered in exasperation: "I'm on my way to eternity, and I know why!"

Saint Margaret Mary Alacoque (1645–1690) was a French mystic and nun of the Visitation order whose visions led eventually to the church's adoption of devotions to the Sacred Heart of Jesus. As she was dying she said: "I need nothing but God and to lose myself in the heart of Jesus."

Saint Gemma Galgani (1878–1903) was a young Italian visionary and stigmatist who offered herself to God as a "victim soul" for the salvation of others. Dying of tuberculosis of the spine, which she bore with heroic holiness, she said: "I seek for nothing more; I have made the sacrifice of everything and of everyone to God; now I prepare to die." She gasped, "Now it is indeed true that nothing more remains to me, Jesus. I recommend my poor soul to you....Jesus!"

Saint Teresa of Jesus (Avila) (1515–1582) was a Spanish Carmelite reformer, mystic and doctor of the church. When the vicar provincial begged her to pray that God would not yet take her away, she replied: "Father, be quiet! Can it be you speaking like that? I am no longer necessary in this world."

Servant of God Matilde Salem (1904–1961) was a Syrian philanthropist, Franciscan tertiary and associate of the Salesians who gave her life to serving the poor. Having donated her own home for the care of children, she was able to say as she lay dying of cancer: "I die in a house that is no longer my own."

Pierre Pigneau de Behaine (1741–1799) was a French bishop and missionary to Vietnam. At the end of his life, he wrote: "I willingly leave this world where I have been thought happy in that I have had public admiration, been respected by the great, esteemed by kings. I can't say that I regret all these honors—it's just that they add up to vanity and trouble."

Mary Stuart (1542–1587), Queen of Scots, was the last Catholic ruler of Scotland. Just before her execution at Queen Elizabeth's command, she told her attendants: "You ought to rejoice and not to weep, for the end of all Mary Stuart's troubles is now come. You know that all this world is but vanity and full of trouble and sorrow."

Junípero Serra (1713–1784), known as the "Father of California," was a Spanish Franciscan missionary to the native peoples of what is now the western United States. He died whispering: "Now I shall rest."

Francis Albert (Frank) Sinatra (1915–1998), the popular American entertainer, said to his wife just before he died: "I'm losin'."

Frédéric Chopin on his deathbed said to his doctors: "Let me die. Don't keep me longer in this world of exile. Let me die. Why do you prolong my life when I have renounced all things and God has enlightened my soul? God calls me; why do you call me back?"

Margaret of Scotland (c. 1419–1445) was rejected by her husband, the future Louis XI of France, because she was unable to bear him any children. Dying of pneumonia, she exclaimed: "Fie on the life of this world! Do not speak to me more about it!"

Sebastien-Roch Nicolas (1741–1794) was a French writer and wit who took the name Chamfort. He wrote just before his death: "Ah, my friend, at last I am about to leave this world, where the heart must be broken or be brass."

Venerable Marie of the Incarnation (1599–1672) was an Ursuline missionary to Quebec. To the children she had taught, gathered around her deathbed, she said: "There, now, a grave isn't anything to worry about. Didn't you know that it's only a place for old clothes?"

Saint Thomas More (1478–1535), chancellor of England and a famed Renaissance scholar, refused to sign King Henry VIII's Act of Supremacy—an act that severed the Church of England from Rome. Imprisoned in the Tower of London, awaiting his execution, he wrote a final prayer that included these words:

> Give me Your grace, good Lord, to count the world as nothing; to set my mind firmly on You and not to hang on the blasting words of men's mouths; to be content to be solitary; not to long for worldly company; little and little to cast off the world utterly, and rid my mind of all the world's business; not to long to hear of any worldly

things, but to find that hearing about worldly delusions is unpleasant to me...to abstain from empty conversation, to avoid frivolous, foolish mirth and gladness; to cut off unnecessary recreations; to consider as nothing the loss of worldly goods, friends, liberty, life and all, for the sake of winning Christ.

Saint Catherine of Siena (1347–1380), the Italian Dominican tertiary, visionary and doctor of the church, practiced the discipline of detachment even from childhood. At the end she summed up her life this way: "I have not sought vainglory, but only the glory and praise of God!"

FIVE

"Father, Forgive Them"

FORGIVENESS

> *Then Jesus said, "Father,*
> *forgive them; for they do*
> *not know what they are*
> *doing."*
> —Luke 23:34

IN JESUS' FAMILIAR PARABLE ABOUT THE UNGRATEFUL servant, those who fail to forgive are compared to tortured prisoners (see Matthew 18:21–35). Resentment, bitterness, the bearing of a grudge—all these are a kind of bondage, handcuffs that chain us emotionally and spiritually to those who have offended us. We languish in the prison cells of our hearts, miserably tormented by the anger seething within.

Not surprisingly, then, one of the Greek words of the Gospel text that we translate "to forgive" means literally "to let go" or "to release." So Jesus' instructions "Forgive, and you will be forgiven" (Luke 6:37) might be more vividly translated "Let go, and you yourself will be released." Only when we're willing to let go of an offense against us and lay it down for good are we ourselves set free.

For this reason, forgiveness is an essential form of the spiritual detachment so necessary to anyone who hopes to live, and to die, in peace. That's why the age-old Catholic rituals for the dying wisely include a pointed query from the attending priest about whether all enemies have been forgiven, all offenses let go. Jesus warns us: "If you do not forgive others, neither will your Father forgive your trespasses" (Matthew 6:15). At the hour of death, when we prepare to face our Judge, dare we give him any reason to deny us mercy?

Even so, hard experience teaches us just how formidable a task it can be to forgive our enemies. When the offender shows no remorse or when the offense has cost us severely—a permanent disability, perhaps, or the loss of a loved one—we may find ourselves crying out to God for the grace to pardon when everything in us demands revenge.

When we do turn to him for help, we find that our Lord himself has given us an example full of courage and strength. Could any injury against us possibly be greater than the injuries he endured? Yet when his agony was sharpest, he cried out in words that must have stunned and pierced his murderers: "Father, forgive them."

The lives and deaths of his followers have echoed that thrilling scene, beginning with Saint Stephen. Not long after the Day of Pentecost, when the church was still young, he was stoned for preaching the gospel. "He knelt down and cried out in a loud voice, 'Lord, do not hold this sin against them'" (Acts 7:60). Those words became the dying declaration of Christian martyrs in every age—and the prayer of every believer who hopes for true freedom in this world and the next.

* * *

Saint James the Lesser (d. 62), one of the twelve apostles, was a leader among the first Christians in Jerusalem and, according to one tradition, a kinsman of Jesus. He was thrown from the pinnacle of the temple and then stoned to death for preaching the gospel. As he died he prayed: "I beg you, O Lord God, Father, forgive them, for they know not what they do."

Saint James the Greater (d. 44), another of the twelve apostles, testified to his Lord at his trial before King Herod Agrippa. According to tradition, the informer who had denounced him as a Christian was converted to Christ by the apostle's faith and was himself condemned. On the way to their execution, the man asked forgiveness of James, who embraced him and said: "Peace be with you, brother."

Saint Wenceslas (907–929), king of Bohemia, promoted the Christian faith in his realm. Murdered by his pagan brother, he said as he died: "May God forgive you, brother."

Charles III (1716–1788), king of Spain, was asked on his deathbed whether he forgave his enemies. He replied: "I did not need this extremity to forgive them. They were forgiven the moment they injured me."

Saint Maria Goretti (1890–1902) died at age eleven after being stabbed while resisting a would-be rapist who was sixteen years old. While she lay in the hospital dying of her wounds, the attending priest asked, "Do you forgive your murderer with all your heart?"

She answered: "Yes, I too, for the love of Jesus, forgive him,…and I want him to be with me in paradise.…May God forgive him, because I have already forgiven him."

Saint Thomas More, awaiting execution, reflected on the life of Joseph recounted in the Old Testament. Joseph's brothers sold him into slavery, yet God ultimately used their betrayal to bring great blessing to Joseph and to his people. More wrote just before he died: "Give me your grace, good Lord … to think my greatest enemies my best friends; for the brothers of Joseph could never have done him so much good with their love and favor as they did him with their malice and hatred." On the scaffold More forgave his executioner and gave him gold.

Richard I (1157–1199), king of England, was known as Richard the Lion Heart. When an archer, Betrand de Gourdon, was captured after mortally wounding him with an arrow, the king said: "Young man, I forgive you. Take off his chains, give him one hundred shillings and let him go."

Catherine of Aragon (1485–1536) became queen of England as the first of Henry VIII's many wives. Henry divorced her, separated her from her daughter and imprisoned her. With the rest of the church, she never recognized the divorce as valid.

Catherine wrote in a last letter to Henry:

My most dear lord, king and husband,
The hour of my death now drawing on, the tender love I
owe you [compels me to advise you to look to]…the
health and safeguard of your soul which you ought to prefer before all worldly matters, and before the care and
pampering of your body, for the which you have cast me
into many calamities and yourself into many troubles.
For my part, I pardon you everything, and I wish to
devoutly pray God that He will pardon you also.

Louis I the Pious (778–840), emperor of the Franks, was
the son of Charlemagne. He died while trying to put
down a rebellion led by one of his sons, of whom he said:
"I pardon him, but let him know that it is on his account
that I am dying."

Engelbert Dolfuss (1892–1934), an Austrian chancellor
who was mortally wounded by Nazi gunmen, said to the
policemen who came to his aid: "I only wanted peace. We
never attacked; we only had to defend ourselves. May the
Lord forgive them."

Henry III (1551–1589), king of France, was mortally
wounded by a Dominican friar in the religious and political turmoil that characterized his reign. When asked by the
priest whether he forgave his enemies, he answered: "I forgive them with all my heart." When asked whether that
included the assassin and his colleagues, he said: "Yes,
even them. I pray to God that he may pardon them their
sins as I hope he will pardon mine."

Louis XIII heard laughter in a nearby room on the day he died of tuberculosis. He told the priest that he suspected his wife was unfaithful. The priest scolded him for thinking such thoughts, and Louis replied: "In my present condition I am obliged to forgive her, but I am not obliged to believe her."

Saint Protasius (d. second century) and his twin brother, Saint Gervasius, suffered martyrdom for their faith in one of the early Roman imperial persecutions of the church, as did their parents before them. Protasius said to his persecutor: "I bear you no anger...for I know that you are blind in your heart. Instead I pity you, for you don't know what you're doing. Don't stop torturing me, so I may share with my brother the sight of our Master's good face."

Pope Pius VI (1717–1799) was imprisoned by Napoleon when the French emperor conquered the papal states. Pius refused to turn his temporal power over to his captor and died in prison in France, praying: "Lord, forgive them."

Mary Stuart, Queen of Scots, told the executioner: "I forgive you with all my heart, for now I hope you shall make an end of all my troubles."

SIX

"I Am Thirsty"
H u m i l i t y

> *After this, when Jesus*
> *knew that all was now*
> *finished, he said...,*
> *"I am thirsty."*
> —John 19:28

IMAGINE THE SCENE. KNOWING THAT "IT IS IMPOSSIBLE for a prophet to be killed outside of Jerusalem" (Luke 13:33) and that his enemies wait there to kill him, Jesus enters the holy city one last time. A throng of supporters lines his way, according to the ancient custom of welcoming sovereigns, generals and other dignitaries. They hail him as the royal son of David, who was Israel's most illustrious ruler (see Matthew 21:1–9). And a king he is—the "King of kings" himself (Revelation 19:16).

Some of his followers are wealthy; if he desired, he could secure a fine horse to make his appearance. But he chooses instead a more modest approach, fulfilling the Scripture: "Look, your king is coming to you, humble, and mounted on a donkey" (Matthew 21:5; see Zechariah 9:9). No doubt those who watch from a distance, jealous or afraid of him, snicker as he rides by.

Yet little do his adversaries realize the truth of the matter: even if our Lord were entering the city with the entire imperial Roman court and army in his train, mounted on a magnificent throne as lord of the world, he still would be humbling himself beyond all telling. For no title, no palace, no majesty on earth, could begin to match the glory he has laid aside simply to become a man and live among us.

A few days later, at the hour of his death, the abyss of that divine humility opens up before us. Saint Paul marveled:

> Christ Jesus,…
> though he was in the form of God,
>> did not regard equality with God
>> as something to be exploited,
> but emptied himself,
>> taking the form of a slave,
>> being born in human likeness.
> And being found in human form,
>> he humbled himself
>> and became obedient to the point of death—
>> even death on a cross. (Philippians 2:5–8)

Nowhere is our Lord's humanity—and thus his humility—more evident, more poignant, than in his dying words "I am thirsty." In that simple statement he expresses the weakness to which human nature is subject. In his case the admission is all the more moving because the weakness is self-imposed, freely chosen so that his human brothers and sisters might be rescued from the ravages of the pride that has ruined their race.

In this light Saint Paul insists: "Let the same mind be in you that was in Christ Jesus" (Philippians 2:5). In sharing his humility we find our salvation.

One of the ancient Hebrew words we often translate as "humble" in the Old Testament can also be translated "afflicted." The inner connection of the two meanings should be clear: Those who are lowly have often been brought low by adversity.

Catholic tradition affirms and develops this connection, in two contexts especially. First, we encourage one another to "offer it up" when suffering comes our way, accepting our lot and trusting that pain can be redemptive as long as we allow it to purge us of haughtiness and the pretense of self-sufficiency. Second, we voluntarily take on afflictions, with varying degrees of severity, as a way of humbling ourselves. Abstinence, fasting, vigils and similar kinds of penance are types of mortification—literally, a "putting to death" of arrogant self-will, vanity and disordered attachments to the world.

Other self-imposed penances hurt our bodies less yet inflict pain on our pride through symbolic gestures of humiliation. The reception of ashes at the beginning of Lent, for example, has its roots in the ancient rite of mourning the dead. Penitents once covered themselves with dust and ashes and sat on the ground, grieving over sins as they would grieve over bereavement.

It was a vivid reminder: Every reason they might have to be proud would one day crumble and be trodden underfoot. The words *humble* and *humus,* after all, have the same root, the Latin term for *dirt.* To be lowly is to be near the ground.

At the hour of death, then, we find Catholics embracing humility in various ways. Some gladly confess their smallness before God, their moral failures, their weaknesses. Others humble themselves by joining gesture to word, acting out a final drama of penance through some act of mortification. Still others accept their dying agony as a purging fire. Their last words display a hope that the pain will burn arrogance to ashes; they trust that as death brings them down to the grave, body and soul will each find at last its own proper *humus*. In all these scenes we encounter a reenactment of Jesus' self-humiliation on the cross.

* * *

Louis François Auguste Cardinal de Rohan-Chabot (1788–1833), archbishop of Besançon, France, cried out as he died: "I am nothing, nothing, less than nothing!"

Saint Camillus de Lellis, referring to sins of his youth, said: "I beseech you on my knees to pray for me, for I have been a great sinner, a gambler and a man of bad life."

Saint Martin of Tours chose to lie on a bed of ashes for several days and nights, refusing even the coarsest blanket, saying: "It is not fitting for a Christian to die otherwise than lying upon ashes, and if I gave you any other example, I should be sinning."

Charles-Louis de Secondat (1689–1755), Baron de Montesquieu, was a French political philosopher who ended with the words: "I am conscious of the greatness of God and the littleness of man."

Frédéric Chopin spoke to God at the end about his musical compositions. "Without you I would have grunted like a pig!"

Vincenzo Bellini (1801–1835) was a Sicilian composer famed for his operas. He said wistfully at the end: "Perhaps someday they will hear my music without even saying, 'Poor Bellini!'"

Pierre Simon Laplace (1749–1827) was a brilliant French astronomer, mathematician and physicist. With his last words he admitted: "What we know is of small amount; what we do not know is enormous."

Blessed Miguel of Ecuador (1854–1910), one of the de la Salle Christian Brothers, was a young and brilliant scholar, writer and poet who contracted pneumonia. When told that he couldn't die before finishing his work, he replied: "If the work I am doing is useful for God, he will send someone else to finish it, and it will be done better than I could do it."

Gabriel Fauré (1845–1924), the French composer and organist, told his sons a day would come when his work would be ignored. But he urged them not to be distressed about it: "There is always a moment of oblivion. All that is unimportant. I did what I could. May God be the judge."

Charles VII (1403–1461), king of France, observed on his deathbed that it was the feast of Saint Mary Magdalene, who in that time was widely believed to be a penitent prostitute. Then he added: "I thank God that I, the greatest of sinners, should die on this day."

Saint Pambo (d. c. 390), one of the desert fathers in ancient Egypt, was mentored by Saint Antony the Great. His last words: "Since I came into the desert, I have eaten nothing that I have not earned by work, and I do not remember that I have ever said anything for which I had need to be sorry afterward. Nevertheless, I must now go to God before I have even begun to serve him."

Blessed Brother André Bessette (1845–1937), known as the "Miracle Worker of Montreal," Canada, took temporary vows with the Holy Cross Fathers and was founder and guardian of the Oratory of Saint Joseph. Numerous cures were reported as a result of his prayers. He often said of himself: "I am ignorant. If there were anyone more ignorant, the good God would have chosen him in my place." As he was dying of acute gastritis, he asked his religious superior: "Pray for my conversion."

Pope Gregory XV (1554–1623) vigorously resisted the Protestant Reformation. He told the cardinals gathered around his deathbed: "I shall die with one consolation. ... No matter who is chosen, my beloved brothers, my successor will necessarily be more worthy of the authority than I am, and better qualified to fill the exalted pontifical office."

Pope Gregory XVI (1765–1846) had belonged to the strict Camaldolese order before his election. As he lay dying he insisted: "I wish to die as a monk and not as a sovereign."

Alexandre Dumas (1802–1870), author of *The Count of Monte Cristo* and *The Three Musketeers*, said to his son of the same name: "Tell me, Alexandre, on your soul and conscience, do you believe that anything of mine will live?"

Ronald Knox (1888–1957) was an English monsignor and apologist, best known for his translation of the Bible. When someone offered to read to him from his translation, he answered: "No. Awfully jolly of you to suggest it, though."

Saint Patrick (c. 389–461) was a British-born missionary priest and bishop whose efforts led to the transformation of Ireland and earned him the title "Apostle to the Irish." In his *Confession,* authored late in life, he wrote:

> I pray that those who believe and fear God, whoever deigns to look at or receive this writing which Patrick, a sinner, unlearned, has composed in Ireland, that no one should ever say that it was my ignorance if I did or showed forth anything however small according to God's good pleasure; but let this be your conclusion and let it so be thought, that—as is the perfect truth—it was the gift of God. This is my confession before I die.

Saint Teresa of Jesus (Avila) said to her spiritual daughters in the convent as she lay dying: "Don't imitate the bad example this nun has given you, and forgive me."

Élisabeth Bruyère (1818–1876) was a Canadian educator who founded the Sisters of Charity of Ottawa and dedicated her life to serving the poor and the sick. Dying from a tumor, she presented her final instructions to her sisters: "Greater mortification…Greater humility…With a lot of good will, we can accomplish much."

Saint Cajetan of Thiene (1480–1547) was an Italian scholar-priest and founder of the Theatines. Urged to lie on a mattress as he was dying, he replied: "My Savior died on a cross. Allow me at least to die on wood."

Lorenzo Giustiniani (1381–1456), patriarch of Venice, replied to attendants who wanted to place him in a more comfortable bed: "My Savior did not die on a featherbed, but on the hard wood of the cross!"

Saint Louis Orione, recovering from two strokes before he died from a third, was found sitting up and trying to pare the corns off his knees, which had developed because of his long hours in prayer. Louis remarked: "I don't know what will happen to this old body, but I want to get rid of these things before I die. We don't want a lot of people to see them and start making something of it."

Ferdinand I (c. 1380–1416), king of Aragon, humbled himself as he was dying by having his attendants remove his royal crown and robe, then lay him on the floor, with ashes scattered on his head. He prayed: "You are the King of kings, the Supreme One both in heaven and on earth. I return to you the crown that you have given me, which I have worn through your great pleasure; and now I only ask that when my soul leaves this body, you will receive me into your celestial mansion."

William Longsword (d. c. 942), duke of Normandy, ordered his body to be laid in a stone coffin and placed under the eaves outside a chapel rather than buried. That way, he said, "the drippings of the rain from the roof may wash my bones as I lie, and cleanse them from the impurity contracted in my sinful and neglected life."

Jean-Baptiste Lully died with a halter around his neck as a sign of penance, singing with tears of remorse and agony: "Sinner, you must die."

Saint Dominic de Guzmán (1170–1221) was the Spanish priest, preacher and reformer who founded the Order of Preachers (Dominicans). When asked where he wished to be buried, he replied: "Under the feet of my friars."

Saint Padre Pio, known for his great holiness, said to a fellow priest: "Son, if the Lord calls me tonight, ask all my brothers to forgive me for all the trouble that I have caused them, and ask all our fellow priests and my spiritual children to say a prayer for my soul."

SEVEN

"Why Have You Forsaken Me?"

CRIES FOR MERCY

> *And about three o'clock*
> *Jesus cried with a loud*
> *voice,* "Eli, Eli, lema
> sabachthani?" *that is,*
> *"My God, my God, why*
> *have you forsaken me?"*
> —Matthew 27:46

PERHAPS THE MOST DISTURBING OF JESUS' LAST WORDS from the cross is the cry of agony that seems to imply he has been abandoned by his heavenly Father. How could this be? Weren't the divine Father and Son always in perfect fellowship?

We may never understand fully the depths of that cry or its meaning. Yet we begin to catch a glimpse into the mystery when we recognize that in his hour of death, Jesus was quoting the Scripture—the ancient Psalm 22, composed by his royal ancestor David when he also was in distress. That sorrowful text foreshadows in several places the details of the crucifixion: Mocking enemies are gathered around the victim (vv. 6–8, 12); he undergoes severe suffering, with his hands and feet pierced (vv. 14–16); his clothing is divided and taken as a gambling prize (v. 18); and his bones are left unbroken (v. 17).

Our Lord's terrifying lament is in fact the first line of this mournful psalm. So with this startling question he is echoing, confirming, taking on himself, David's shout of anguish, his cry for mercy. And in doing so he shows himself drinking the cup of human misery to the dregs.

The ancient fathers of the church saw here an indication of just how closely united Jesus is with his people. He is the Head of the church (see Ephesians 5:23); we are his body (1 Corinthians 12:27). In this cry, they said, the Head was speaking on behalf of the whole body, giving us all a voice, storming heaven for us—because we who are broken desperately need the pardon of God.

In their own ways Catholics throughout the centuries have echoed that cry for mercy at the hour of death. As death humbles them, they see themselves more clearly; they come to recognize more than ever that they are lost without divine clemency. So they pray for grace for themselves and, often, for their enemies and for the whole world.

Some of the people quoted here need little explanation of why they would beg for mercy on their deathbeds. Their evil deeds obviously left a great burden of guilt on their souls. Even so, their prayers give us hope that no sin is too great for our Father to forgive if our repentance is sincere.

Others cited here we know to be saints, holy men and women who spent their lives serving God and others. In their cries for pardon, we're reminded that none of us are faultless, that all of us depend utterly on divine grace. They teach us that we shouldn't wait until the last

moment to examine our consciences and seek reconciliation with God: "now is the acceptable time" (2
Corinthians 6:2) to ask for his grace and to find it in the
sacraments.

The scriptural warning rings down the ages: "Today, if
you hear his voice, do not harden your hearts" (Hebrews
3:7–8; see Psalm 95:7–8). Tomorrow may be too late.

* * *

Marie Thérèse Charlotte (1778–1851), duchess of
Angoulême, was the last surviving child of King Louis
XVI and Marie Antoinette, who had been assassinated in
the French Revolution. She prayed: "God, I ask pardon
for my sins. Assist your humble servant in this moment
that will decide her eternity."

Mary Stuart, Queen of Scots, knelt down on a cushion
before the beheading block and prayed: "Even as your
arms, O Jesus, were spread upon the cross, so receive me
into your arms of mercy and forgive me all my sins."

Saint Catherine of Siena, after receiving the last rites,
prayed repeatedly: "I have sinned, O Lord; have mercy
upon me! Holy God, have mercy upon me!"

Blessed Marie-Rose Durocher (1811–1849), Canadian educator and founder of the Sisters of the Holy Names of Jesus and Mary, composed a farewell during one of the sleepless nights of her final illness, which reads in part: "I beg pardon, my sisters, for lacking sweetness and kindness in your regard. I beg pardon for having hurt anyone in conversation at recreation, for having spoken harsh or offensive words. I beg pardon for having lacked charity in not having toward you the heart of a mother. I beg pardon for my irregularities in spiritual exercises. I beg pardon for my shortcomings."

Blaise Pascal (1623–1662), the French mathematician and philosopher, said simply: "My God, do not forsake me."

Charles IX (1550–1574), king of France, ordered the infamous Massacre of Saint Bartholomew's Eve in 1572, in which thousands of Protestants were butchered. Dying of tuberculosis, he groaned to his Protestant nurse: "Blood, blood, rivers of blood! So much blood! Ah, nurse, what bad advice I listened to! Ah, God forgive me! I don't know where I am anymore. What will become of me and my people? I am lost, lost! Thank God I have no son to succeed me!"

When asked to transact some item of business, he replied: "It doesn't matter. Nothing on earth matters anymore."

After making his confession and receiving Communion, he prayed: "If only Jesus my Savior would number me among his redeemed!"

Alphonse (Al) Capone (1899–1947) was the American gangster nicknamed "Scarface" who ordered the infamous Saint Valentine's Day Massacre against a rival gang in Chicago. His tombstone reads: "My Jesus Mercy."

Edward II (1284–1327), king of England, was forced to abdicate and later was brutally murdered. His last words: "I thank you, O Lord, for all your benefits. With all my power I ask for your mercy, that you will forgive me for all the sins that I, in my wrongdoing, have committed against you. And I ask with my whole heart the grace of pardon from all men whom I have knowingly or unwittingly offended."

Edward III (1312–1377), king of England, began the Hundred Years' War with France. Deserted at the end by his courtiers and mistress, he was left to die with a single priest, who said to him, "You have sinned terribly against God, and you need to ask his mercy."

Edward whispered in Latin: "Jesus, have mercy." When asked by the priest whether he forgave his enemies, he gestured that he did. And when the priest held out the crucifix, the king pressed it to his lips and died.

Desiderius Erasmus (1466–1536), the Dutch Renaissance scholar and religious writer, cried out after a lingering illness: "Lord, free me! Lord, pity me! Lord, bring the end! Lord, have mercy! Dear God!"

Blessed Mariam of Jesus Crucified (1846–1878) was a Palestinian Carmelite nun and mystic. Dying of gangrene from a broken arm, she prayed: "Oh, yes, mercy!"

Walker Percy (1916–1990), the American novelist, urged his friends as he lay dying from prostate cancer: "Don't ask the Lord to keep me here. Ask him to have mercy."

Ethel Waters (1896–1977), the African-American singer and actress, died after a prolonged illness. Just before her last breath, she called out: "Merciful Father! Precious Jesus!"

Blessed Zélie Martin (1831–1877) was a French lay-woman, the mother of Saint Thérèse of Lisieux. She said as she was dying: "O you who have created me, have mercy on me!"

Saint Francis of Paola (c. 1416–1507), the Italian hermit who founded the Minim Friars, made his final prayer: "O my Lord Jesus Christ! O Good Shepherd, save the just, reclaim sinners, have mercy on all the faithful, living and dead, and on me, a miserable sinner."

Andronicus I Comnenus (c. 1118–1185) was an Eastern Roman emperor who killed his coemperor and instigated a massacre of Westerners in his capital city of Constantinople. Just before his death at the hands of a mob, he shouted: "O Lord, have mercy! Why will you break a bruised reed?"

Hans Frank (1900–1946), Nazi governor general of Poland, was a German war criminal condemned to death by hanging at the Nuremburg trials. He became Catholic after his arrest and was the only one of the condemned to enter the execution chamber with a smile on his face, apparently relieved at the prospect of atoning for his crimes.

He lamented: "A thousand years will pass, and the guilt of Germany will not be erased." When asked for any last statement, he replied, "I am thankful for the kind of treatment I received during my captivity, and I ask God to accept me with mercy."

EIGHT

"Believe in God"
FAITH

> *Do not let your hearts be*
> *troubled. Believe in God,*
> *believe also in me.*
> —John 14:1

JESUS KNEW THAT HIS CRUCIFIXION WOULD PUT HIS followers' faith to the ultimate test. Those who still clung to dreams that, as the promised Messiah, he would overthrow the social and political order would be disillusioned. Those who hoped that his life-giving spiritual truth would be embraced by the entire nation, even the hostile religious authorities, would be dismayed. Those who loved him deeply as their master, teacher and best friend would be crushed and even tempted to despair. And all would be terrified that they too, as his disciples, might be the next to suffer such a fate.

On the night Jesus was betrayed he took great pains to instruct his apostles about how to survive the days to come. He made sure to include among his last words a solemn exhortation to hold on to the faith that would be so severely tested.

Despite the fear and confusion, he told them, despite the grief and despair, take heart: "Do not let your hearts be troubled, and do not let them be afraid" (John 14:27).

At the same time he warned them that the enemy of their souls would take this opportunity to assail them, trying with all his might to undermine their faith: "Satan has demanded to sift all of you like wheat, but I have prayed for you" (Luke 22:31–32). They could win the struggle, he assured them, because he would fight with them and through them: "Take courage; I have conquered the world!" (John 16:33).

Ever since that night these words of Jesus have helped to sustain Christians in their last hour. Whether facing martyrdom, as most of the apostles did, or a death in more natural circumstances, they have recalled their Lord's command to believe despite the pain they suffered or the questions that remained unanswered. Many professed their faith one last time in the One who is worthy of all their trust.

We should note here that the church has always spoken of faith as more than mere intellectual assent, the *yes* of the head. It demands as well a commitment of the will, the *yes* of the heart (see James 2:17–19). Catholic faith involves not just accepting certain truths but also embracing a Person, Truth himself, and serving him. Thus many Catholics have died with simply the name of Jesus on their lips, including Saint Aloysius Gonzaga, Saint Vincent de Paul, Saint Robert Bellarmine and Spanish explorer Francisco Pizarro.

The final statements in this chapter reflect both aspects of faith. Some of the dying choose to recite or to echo the words of the Creed, reaffirming one last time the glorious realities that have shaped them in this life and now offer them hope in the next. Others speak more inti-mately of God, in the Person of Father, Son or Holy Spirit. They display a simple loving devotion, a trust that they remain, as they have always been, in the hands of the One who loved them into being and now loves them into eternity.

We also know that faith in Christ implies faith in his church—the body and bride through which he works in the world until his return in glory (see 1 Corinthians 12:12–27; Ephesians 5:25–32). Some of these dying dec-larations, then, express the Catholic faith through a confi-dence in the efficacy of the church's sacraments, the truth of its doctrine, the rightness of its moral teaching, the finality of its authority. Despite the failures of its leaders—and most were well acquainted with such failures—the dying faithful were confident, as missionary Jeanne Mance proclaimed, that they belonged to the church as their mother for their "whole life and all eternity."

* * *

Saint Justin Martyr (c. 100–166) was a Samaritan philosopher who became a Christian and apologist for the faith. He was arrested during a Roman imperial persecu-tion of the church. Before he and his companions were led away to be scourged and beheaded, the Roman prefect asked with a sneer, "Do you really suppose that you will ascend to heaven to receive a reward?"

"No," answered Saint Justin, "I don't suppose it. Rather, I know it and I am fully persuaded of it."

Saint Robert Francis Bellarmine (1542–1621) was an Italian Jesuit cardinal archbishop, theologian and doctor of the church. His apologetic works, which helped to shape the Catholic Reformation, responded brilliantly to the doctrinal challenges of the Protestant Reformers. Dying with a fever, he recited the Apostle's Creed entirely, which ends fittingly with a statement about his coming reward: "I believe ... in the life everlasting. Amen."

Elizabeth Charlotte (seventeenth century), duchess of Orléans, was the sister-in-law of King Louis XIV. She wrote in a letter: "Thank God, I am prepared to die, and I only pray for strength to die bravely. ... Should this be the end, I die with full faith in my Redeemer."

Georges d'Amboise (1460–1510), a French cardinal archbishop and chief minister of state under King Louis XII, died declaring simply: "I believe."

Pope John Paul II (1920–2005), whose teachings, travels and personal charisma transformed the modern papacy, wrote one last homily for Divine Mercy Sunday (a feast he had established), on whose vigil he died. Read in churches and published posthumously, it ended with the proclamation: "The One whom the Virgin bore in her womb, who suffered and died for us, is truly risen. Alleluia!"

Saint John Bosco founded the the Salesians to care for poor and neglected boys and the Daughters of Our Lady, Help of Christians to care for girls in similar circumstances. As death approached at the end of a prolonged illness, he shouted encouragements to his boys even in moments of delirium: "Pray! Pray, but with faith—with living faith! Courage, courage! Onward, ever onward!"

Saint Peter of Verona (1206–1252), also known as Saint Peter the Martyr, was an Italian Dominican preacher who evangelized nearly the whole of Italy. Because he vigorously opposed the Cathari heresy, some of its adherents plotted his murder. Ambushing him on the highway, the assassins struck him with an axe on the head, and he fell to the ground. Though gravely injured, he rose to his knees and recited the first article of the Apostles' Creed. Then, offering his blood as a sacrifice to God, he dipped his fingers in it and wrote on the ground the words: "I believe in God." The murderers then pierced his heart.

Legrand D'Alleray (d. c. 1794) was an aged Frenchman brought before the tribunal with his wife on a trumped-up charge during the Reign of Terror in the French Revolution. When the presiding judge hinted that D'Alleray should offer an evasive reply to save their lives, he replied with loyalty to the moral standards of his faith: "Thank you for the efforts you make to save me, but it would be necessary to purchase our lives by a lie. My wife and I prefer rather to die. We have grown old together without ever having lied, and we will not do it now to save a remnant of life."

Jacques-Bénigne Bossuet (1627–1704), bishop of Meaux, was a French preacher, historian and theologian. He prayed: "Lord, I suffer terribly, but I am not confounded, for I know in whom to trust. Your will be done."

Edmund Husserl (1859–1938) was a German Jewish phenomenological philosopher who deeply influenced Saint Teresa Benedicta of the Cross (Edith Stein) and converted to the Catholic faith during his final illness. On his deathbed on Good Friday, he exclaimed: "Good Friday! What a day! Christ has forgiven us everything!"

Louis XVII (1785–1795), dauphin of France, was the only surviving son of the assassinated King Louis XVI and Marie Antoinette. At the age of ten he was dying of tuberculosis, yet French revolutionaries cast him into prison. He replied to an attendant who expressed grief at seeing him suffer: "Be comforted. I shall not always suffer."

Saint Francis de Sales (1567–1622), bishop of Geneva, Switzerland, and a popular apologist and spiritual writer, was asked as he was dying whether he was afraid of Satan. He replied: "I place all my trust in the Lord, who will know how to deliver me from all my enemies."

Shave Head (d. 1890) was a Sioux policeman of the American Northwest who was mortally wounded in an effort to arrest Sitting Bull, who also died in the attempt. He insisted: "I will die in the faith of the white man and to which my five children already belong, and be with them. Send for my wife, that we may be married by the Black Gown [priest] before I die." By the time his wife arrived a few moments later, he had died in the arms of the priest.

Blessed Daniel Comboni (1831–1881) was a missionary priest to sub-Saharan Africa and founder of the Congregation of the Sons of the Sacred Heart. A few days before he died of typhoid fever, he wrote an associate, commenting on the recent loss of several fellow missionaries to the same disease: "God's works have always been born and grow like this. The church was founded on the blood of the God-Man, and of the apostles and martyrs. All the Catholic missions in the world that have borne fruit have done so in the midst of death, of sacrifice, and in the shade of the saving tree of the cross."

Saint Teresa of Jesus (Avila) kept repeating as she lay dying: "Lord, I am a daughter of the church....I am a daughter of the church."

Blessed Ghebre Michael (c. 1790–1855) was an Ethiopian Coptic monk who became a Catholic priest, though he knew that decision might cost him his life. As he was being scourged with giraffe tails, he declared in a loud voice: "I believe in the faith of the holy church, catholic, apostolic and Roman! O my God, I beg you to assist me by your grace and receive me in your great mercy!"

Napoleon Bonaparte (1769–1821), the Italian-Corsican general who became emperor of the French, had numerous conflicts with the church during his tempestuous career; he did not scruple even to imprison a pope. But his last will and testament, written in exile not long before he died, began with this declaration of faith: "I die in the apostolical Roman religion, in the bosom of which I was born, more than fifty years since."

Francis William (Frank) Murphy (1890–1949) was an American statesman who served as governor of Michigan, United States attorney general and Supreme Court justice. Dying of a heart attack, he asked a question that—considering how it reflects the priorities in his mind—perhaps answers itself: "Have I kept the faith?"

Claude-Fredric Bastiat (1801–1850) was a French political economist who became a Catholic just before he died. His last words were a simple credo: "I see, I know, I believe; I am a Christian."

Giuseppe Mazzini (1807–1872), an Italian revolutionary leader who had long declared God to be something of a "geometric solution," woke briefly after three days in a coma, sat up and cried out: "Yes! Yes! I believe in God!" Then he fell back dead.

Jean Racine suffered a long, debilitating sickness. When his son reminded him that the physicians said he would recover, he answered: "Let them have their say. We are not going to contradict them. But, my son, would you too deceive me? Are you too in the conspiracy? Believe me that God alone is master of the event."

Saint John Chrysostom (344–407), a Syrian patriarch of Constantinople and doctor of the church, was renowned for his preaching. He was banished from the city after publicly denouncing the immorality of the imperial capital and court. Dying in exile, he proclaimed jubilantly: "Glory be to God for all things!"

Louis VIII (1187–1226), king of France, lay dying of dysentery, and superstitious courtiers brought a young girl to his bedside, believing he would be cured by having sex with a virgin. Trusting in the moral teaching of the church, he said to the girl: "Ah, no! It will not be so, young lady! I will not commit mortal sin for whatever reason!"

Mary Ann Long (1946–1959), an American girl disfigured by cancer, spent her final days under the care of the Dominican Servants of Relief in Atlanta. A self-styled faith healer came to visit and greeted her with the words, "The Lord Jesus can heal you, Mary Ann!" She replied: "I know Jesus can heal me. I know he can do anything. It doesn't make a bit of difference whether he heals me or not. That's his business."

Saint Joan of Arc (1412–1431) was a French peasant teenager who led her country's troops to victory over the English at Orleans, helping secure the freedom they had lost during the Hundred Years' War. Captured by the English, she cried out as she burned at the stake, "Hold the cross high so I may see it through the flames!" She died with the name of Jesus on her lips.

Saint Theodore (c. 602–690), one of the early archbishops of Canterbury, England, made this dying declaration of faith: "With my Christ I was, and am, and will be!"

Charles Baudelaire (1821–1867), the French poet, said: "Holy name, O holy name!"

Saint Rose of Lima (1586–1617), a Peruvian Dominican tertiary and mystic, at the end prayed: "Jesus, be with me."

Jeanne Mance (1606–1673) was one of the five French cofounders of Montreal, Canada, and the first lay nurse in North America. She served as a missionary to the Native Americans in Quebec and eventually wore herself out through her efforts. The prologue to her last will and testament declares:

> I proclaim that I live and die in the true faith of the holy
> Church, catholic, apostolic, and Roman, which I hold and
> recognize as the only true Church, outside of which there
> is no salvation. I believe and approve all that it approves,
> and I renounce that which it renounces. I revere and

honor and recognize the Church as my one true Mother, vowing an entire and perfect obedience as its true daughter for my whole life and all eternity.

Annie Zelikova (1924–1941), a Czechoslovakian teenager known as "the apostle of the smile," died from tuberculosis. On her deathbed she told a visitor, "I must smile to my last breath. Ah, all I can give God now are my heartbeats and my smile. Nothing is left to me except love and trust." At the very end she smiled and said slowly: "How beautiful it all is. I wouldn't trade places with anyone. My heart is beating for Jesus. I love him so much.... I trust."

Saint Antoninus of Florence (1389–1459) was a Dominican vicar general, archbishop, theologian and founder of the lay society known as the Good Men of Saint Martin. His last words declared his faith in God's sovereignty and the Christian's share in eternal life: *"Servire Deo regnare est,"* "To serve God is to reign."

NINE

"The World Hates You"
M A R T Y R D O M

*If you belonged to the
world, the world would
love you as its own.
Because you do not belong
to the world, but I have
chosen you out of the
world—therefore the world
hates you.*
—John 15:19

A CHRISTIAN MARTYR IS A FLESH-AND-BLOOD CRUCIFIX.
"By martyrdom," the Second Vatican Council observed,
"a disciple is transformed into an image of his Master, who
freely accepted death on behalf of the world's salvation; he
perfects that image, even to the shedding of blood"
(*Lumen Gentium*, 42).

In the last words of the martyrs, we encounter
Catholics who lived their faith unashamedly, whatever the
cost. They worshipped, they served, they preached Jesus
Christ boldly. They made moral judgments by his universal standards, and they acted and taught accordingly.

The martyrs knew that truth could not be relativized,
and they refused to hide or deny it. They could not in good
conscience "go along to get along," when they knew that
the path others were taking led to misery and damnation.

Is it any wonder that they offended people? They illustrated the scriptural warning that Christ and his gospel are a scandal, a stumbling block, an offense to those who reject him (see 1 Corinthians 1:23; 1 Peter 2:8). And they confirmed the sobering truth of Jesus' words the night before he died: "Because you do not belong to the world...the world hates you" (John 15:19).

The martyrs rebuked ambitious government officials and self-assured cultural elites; the wealthy and the powerful; familiar neighbors and faceless mobs. They publicly denounced political leaders for immoral sexual behavior. They told non-Christians that their religious beliefs were mistaken and their gods false or even demonic. They tried to stop people from engaging in forms of murder and other crimes that the government had legalized.

If we show the same feisty zeal, we too could lose our lives. If that should be our lot, God will grant us the grace to emerge victorious, just as they did. And if the privilege of dying for our faith is not ours to receive, our vocation is nevertheless to display a similar heroic holiness: laying down our lives every day, in matters great and small, for the sake of what is right and true.

Thus imitating the martyrs' courage, their passion for God and their loyalty to the truth, each of us will also become a flesh-and-blood crucifix. "If you endure when you do right and suffer for it, you have God's approval. For to this you have been called, because Christ also suffered for you, leaving you an example, so that you should follow in his steps" (1 Peter 2:20–21).

* * *

Saint Polycarp (c. 69–c. 155) was a disciple of Saint John the apostle and bishop of Smyrna, a city in Asia Minor. He was arrested during a Roman imperial persecution of the church. When the proconsul commanded him to denounce Christ, he replied:

> "Eighty-six years I have now served Christ, and he has never done me the least wrong. How, then, can I blaspheme my Lord and Savior?"
>
> Later the proconsul said to him, "I will have you consumed by fire if you won't change your mind."
>
> Saint Polycarp answered: "You threaten me with fire that burns for a moment, and after a little while is extinguished. But you are ignorant of the fire of the coming judgment and of eternal punishment, reserved for the ungodly. But why delay? Do whatever you want."

Saint Ignatius of Antioch (c. 30–107) was the bishop of Antioch in Syria. According to ancient legend he was a disciple of Saint John and was consecrated bishop by Saint Peter. Arrested during a Roman imperial persecution, he was sent to Rome in chains to be thrown to the wild beasts in the arena. On the way he wrote a letter to the Christians at Rome, asking them not to intervene with the authorities to try to save his life:

> I write to the Churches, and impress on them all, that I will willingly die for God, unless you hinder me. I beg you not to do me an untimely favor. Allow me to become food for the wild beasts, through whom it will be granted me to attain to God.

I am the wheat of God. Let me be ground by the teeth of the wild beasts, that I may be found to be the pure bread of Christ. In fact, encourage the wild beasts, so that they may become my tomb, and may leave nothing of my body. That way, when I have fallen asleep in death, I will be no trouble to anyone. Then I will truly be a disciple of Christ.

Saint Andrew Kim (1821–1846) was a Korean priest, the son and grandson of martyrs for the faith. From prison he wrote a last letter to his people: "You must love and help one another, and wait hopefully for the time when our Lord in his mercy will relieve our sufferings. Whatever happens, behave in such a way that God will be glorified. …Be steadfast, and let us meet in heaven."

After three months in prison, Father Kim was beheaded. Just before his death he preached a farewell homily, declaring: "My eternal life is beginning now."

Saint John Houghton (1487–1535), an English priest and prior of the Carthusian charterhouse in London, became one of the Forty Martyrs of England and Wales because of his refusal to accept King Henry VIII as head of the church. As the torturer was in the act of tearing out his heart, Houghton prayed: "Good Jesu, what will you do with my heart?" His body was chopped into pieces, which were hung in various places around London.

Saint Alban (d. 304) was probably the first Christian martyr of Britain. According to legend, he was executed for being a Christian in the persecution of the Roman Emperor Diocletian. He said to his persecutors, who wanted him to sacrifice to the Roman gods: "These sacrifices, which are offered to devils, are of no avail. Hell is the reward of those who offer them."

Saint Andrew (first century) was one of Jesus' twelve apostles. According to an ancient tradition, he was crucified on an X-shaped cross at Patras, Acaia, for preaching the gospel. He said: "O cross, I welcome you and have long expected you! With a willing mind, with joy and longing, I come to you, for I am the disciple of him who hung on you. I have always been your lover and desired to embrace you!"

Saint Lucy Kim Nusia (1817–1839), a Korean woman who made a lifelong vow of virginity, was arrested, tortured and interrogated because of her faith. While in prison she cut and sold her beautiful hair to buy food, which she shared with her fellow inmates.

Just before she was beheaded, she was asked, "Aren't you afraid to die?" She replied, "Yes, I am afraid to die, but I would rather die than deny my Lord."

When asked whether she had seen God, she answered, "Can a country man who has never seen the king believe that there is a king? When I see all the creatures on earth, I know that there is a Creator."

Saint Thomas Becket (c. 1118–1170), archbishop of Canterbury, England, was murdered in the cathedral by King Henry II's thugs because he refused to subject the church to secular authority. His last words: "Into your hands, O Lord, I commend my spirit! I accept death for the name of Jesus and his church." He slid to the floor, extending his arms to form a cross.

Saint Cyprian (c. 200–258) was a pagan rhetorician, lawyer and teacher of Carthage, North Africa, before becoming a Christian theologian and eventually the first bishop-martyr of Africa. During the persecution of the church by the Roman emperor Valerian, he responded to the judge examining him: "I am a Christian and a bishop. I know no other gods but the one true God, who made heaven and earth, the sea, and all that is in them. It is this God that we Christians serve; to him we pray day and night, for ourselves and all mankind, and for the welfare of the emperors themselves."

When the judge pronounced the death sentence, Cyprian replied: "Praise be to God!"

Saint Apphianus (286–306) was a Palestinian teenager of Caesaria who died during the Roman imperial persecution of Maximinius. Commanded by the authorities to divulge his name, his father's name and his residence, he responded: "I am a Christian. My father is God."

Saint Irene (d. 304) was a Greek woman of Thessalonika arrested for being a Christian in one of the Roman imperial persecutions of the church. When asked by the governor whether she had the rashness to refuse to sacrifice to the Roman gods, she replied: "It is not rashness but godly piety. In that I am firm." She was burned at the stake.

Saint James the Dismembered (d. 421) was a Persian army officer who was sawn alive into twenty-eight pieces for refusing to renounce his faith. Legend tells us that after his limbs were hacked off, he told his executioners: "Now the boughs are gone. Cut down the trunk."

Then he prayed: "O Lord of lords, Lord of the living and the dead, give ear to me who am half dead. I have no fingers to hold out to you, O Lord, nor hands to stretch forth to you. My feet are cut off and my knees demolished, so I cannot bend the knee to you, and I am like a house that is about to fall because its columns are taken away. Hear me, O Lord Jesus Christ, and deliver my soul from its prison!"

Saint Justin Martyr replied to the Roman prefect who threatened to execute him if he didn't sacrifice to the Roman gods: "Even when we have been punished by you, through prayer we can be saved through our Lord Jesus Christ, our Savior. He has guaranteed salvation for us and will give us confidence when we appear before his terrible and universal judgment seat."

Saint Maximilian (273–295) was the son of a veteran of the imperial Roman army who refused military service, saying: "My army is the army of God, and I cannot fight for this world." When the proconsul told him that other Christians were serving in the army, he replied: "That is their business. I am a Christian too, and I cannot serve." He was threatened with execution if he further refused. He insisted: "I shall not die. When I leave this earth, I shall live with Christ, my Lord."

Once he was condemned to beheading, Maximilian urged his father: "Take every measure to merit [a similar] crown [so] that you yourself may soon see God. Give the new uniform you intended for me to the soldier who strikes me."

Saint Perpetua (180–202) was a North African noblewoman condemned to die in the arena at Carthage for refusing to denounce Christ. She tied her hair up as she was led out to face the beasts, saying: "It is not becoming for a martyr to suffer with disheveled hair, lest she appear to be mourning in her glory."

Saint Philip the Apostle (d. c. 90) was martyred, according to tradition, by the Roman governor of Hierapolis in Asia Minor. He prayed as he was crucified: "Clothe me in your glorious robe and the seal of your ever-shining light, until I have passed by all the rulers of the world and our adversary, the evil dragon."

Saint Polycronius (d. 251), a bishop of Babylon, refused to sacrifice to the Roman gods as commanded by Emperor Decius. Just before he was beaten to death, he declared: "We offer ourselves in the Lord Jesus Christ and will not bow to idols made with hands."

Blessed Miguel Pro (1891–1927), a Mexican priest, was arrested by the police of a rabidly anti-Catholic national regime. He faced the firing squad with a crucifix in one hand and a rosary in the other, his arms outstretched like Christ's on the cross, quietly declaring: *"Viva Cristo Rey!"* "Long live Christ the King!"

Saint Theodosia (288–304) was a teenage Palestinian girl arrested in the persecutions of the church under the Roman emperor Diocletian. When she refused to offer incense to the Roman gods, she was raked with iron claws, sealed in a bag and thrown into the sea. According to legend, just before she was drowned, she told her executioners: "Don't you see that I am experiencing what I prayed for: to be found worthy of joining the company of the martyrs of God?"

Thaddeus O'Daly (d. 1577), a Franciscan friar, was one of the Irish Martyrs executed for the faith between 1537 and 1714. He was hanged, drawn and quartered at Limerick. Bystanders reported that his head, severed from his body, said distinctly: "Lord, show me your ways."

Dominic Collins (d. 1602), a Jesuit lay brother and another one of the Irish Martyrs, was hanged at Cork. As he was led to his execution, with his hands tied behind his back and a halter around his neck, he urged his fellow Irish Catholics: "Look up to heaven and, worthy descendants of your ancestors who ever constantly professed it, hold fast to that faith for which I am this day to die."

Saint Maurice (d. c. 287) was an officer of the Theban Legion, composed of Egyptian Christians, in the army of the Roman emperor Maximian Herculius. They refused to sacrifice to the Roman gods to ensure victory in battle, and the emperor had many of them executed near Lake Geneva in what is now Switzerland. Maurice gave this defense to the emperor at his execution: "We are your soldiers, but also the soldiers of the true God. We owe you military service and obedience; but we cannot renounce him who is our Creator and Master, and also yours, even though you reject him.... We have arms in our hands, but we do not resist because we would rather die innocent than live by any sin."

Saint Dionysa (d. 484), a noblewoman of Byzacena (now Tunisia), was tortured and executed for remaining Catholic when the heretical Vandals invaded North Africa. Having been stripped naked, beaten cruelly and displayed publicly, she said: "You servants of the devil, what you think you are doing to my shame is in fact to my praise....The punishment to be feared is the one that will never end, and the life to be desired is the one that will be enjoyed forever."

Saint Joseph Mkasa (1860–1885) was one of the Martyrs of Uganda. A catechist in charge of the pages of King Mwanga, he was beheaded for protecting them from the king's sexual abuse and for denouncing the king's murder of a group of Protestant missionaries. Joseph walked to his death unbound, saying: "Why should you bind me? From whom should I escape? From God? Tell Mwanga that I forgive him for putting me to death without a reason, but let him repent. Otherwise I shall accuse him in God's court."

Saint Noah Mawaggali (1850–1886), another of the Martyrs of Uganda, was the leading catechist of the village of Mityana. He sent all the Christians into hiding from King Mwanga but refused to hide himself, telling his sister: "I know there is another life, and for that reason I am not afraid of losing this one."

Saint Charles Lwanga (d. 1886) succeeded Saint Joseph Mkasa as guardian of the pages of King Mwanga. He said to his fellow martyrs before he was burned at the stake: "My friends, good-bye. We'll meet again in heaven." Then he said to one of his executioners: "How happy I would be if you, too, were to embrace my religion."

Saint Peter Zhu Rixin (1881–1900) was one of the 120 Martyrs of China who were massacred for their faith during the Boxer Rebellion. When the Boxer general tried to persuade him to renounce God, Peter replied: "Would you deny your mother and father? If you would not do that, much less will I deny my Father, my God."

Blessed Anre Phu Yen (1625–1644), a teenage catechist, is considered the proto-martyr of the church in Vietnam. When questioned by the authorities, he declared: "I wish I had a thousand lives to offer to God in thanksgiving for what he has done for me."

Saint Crispina (d. 304) was a noblewoman of Numidia (now Algeria). She was executed by the Roman imperial authorities for refusing to offer incense to the Roman gods. Her final declaration: "I have never sacrificed and I shall not do so save to the one true God and to our Lord, Jesus Christ, his Son, who was born and died.... That religion is worthless...which forces [people] to be crushed against their will.... I do not fear anything you say."

Servant of God Maria de la Luz Camacho (1907–1934), a young Mexican Franciscan tertiary, was shot by soldiers of the anti-Catholic Red Syndicate while barring their entry to a Catholic church they intended to burn down. As they taunted and threatened her, she replied: "We are not afraid. If it becomes necessary, we are ready to die for Christ the King. Those who wish to enter this church must first pass over my body."

Blessed Richard Trouvé of Saint Ann (1568–1617), a Belgian Franciscan missionary to Mexico and Japan, was arrested and condemned to death for his faith by the Japanese authorities in Nagasaki. He wrote to a fellow friar in Belgium: "We religious and those who have helped us are to be burnt at a slow fire; the others will be beheaded....If my mother is still alive, I beg you to be so kind as to tell her of God's mercy to me in allowing me to suffer and die for Him. I have no time left to write to her myself."

Servant of God Blas de Rodríguez (d. 1597) was a Spanish Franciscan priest and missionary to the Guale people of what is now coastal Georgia in the United States. A gang of native assassins began murdering the friars in the area because the priests insisted on monogamy for Christian converts. Before Father Blas was tomahawked, he said to his captors: "My sons, for me it is not difficult to die. Even if you should not cause it, the death of this body is inevitable. We have to be ready at all times, for we, all of us, have to die some day. But what does pain me is that the evil one has persuaded you to do this offensive thing against your God and Creator."

Blessed Juan Bautista (c. 1660–1700) was a Mexican lay leader who refused, along with a companion, to take part in idolatrous ceremonies of the local community in Oaxaca. When a mob threatened to burn the monastery where he had taken refuge, he presented himself to them and said: "We are going to die for the law of God, and since I have no fear of God's divine majesty, I need no weapons." His final words as the mob beat him to death were to ask the other friars to remember him in their prayers to God.

Elias del Socorro Nieves (1882–1928) was a Mexican priest whose government had outlawed the saying of Mass. He forgave and prayed for the soldiers who knelt before him to receive a blessing. The captain executed two of his companions first, then said to Father Elias: "Now it is your turn. Let us see whether dying is like saying Mass." The priest replied: "You have spoken the truth, because to die for the faith is a sacrifice pleasing to God."

TEN

"No One Will Take Your Joy"
H U M O R

> *You have pain now; but I
> will see you again, and
> your hearts will rejoice,
> and no one will take your
> joy from you.*
> —John 16:22

SAINT THOMAS MORE WAS FROM HIS EARLY DAYS A
first-class joker. As a boy he once wrote a stand-up comedy
routine to welcome guests at his parents' feast. His youth-
ful Latin compositions play on the fact that his name in
Greek, *Moros,* means "fool," and they sparkle with wit.

As an adult he became famous for his practical jokes,
such as "medicating" the food of guests—with what kind
of surprises we can only speculate. Even his formal treatises include a number of funny stories whose good
humor can still draw laughter nearly five centuries later. Is
it any wonder that such a man's household included a live-
in professional jester and a pet monkey?

Yet More never shied away from serious matters. So
that the shadow of death would shade his eyes from this
world's dazzling temptations, he arranged to have his
own tomb built and his epitaph engraved in the prime of
his life.

His writings also show his serious side. The somber treatise *The Last Things,* for example, centers on the "four last things" of classical Catholic theology: death, judgment, hell and heaven. Such meditations he found essential for remaining spiritually detached in a life characterized by status and wealth, power and fame. He was, after all, chancellor of England, a prosperous businessman and a respected scholar.

In the end More was imprisoned in the Tower of London for fifteen months and threatened with execution for refusing to recognize King Henry VIII as head of the Church of England. In that gloomy, frightening place the shadow was short: he was now face-to-face with death. Yet even one of the treatises he wrote there was filled with "merry tales," as he called them, and when the time came to approach the gallows, he joked with his executioners.

More is by no means alone in regard to humor at the death knell. Numerous Catholics have found room for jesting at their critical hour. How can we explain this puzzling fact?

Perhaps we need to reconsider the relations between hope and humor. Someone once said that God has given us hope to encourage us about what we can one day become and humor to console us for what we are now. Laughter is, after all, our response to the gap between what is and what should be. So a finely tuned sense of humor is often the distinguishing mark of clear vision—the kind that sees this life sharply with all its incongruities yet sees as well the possibilities and implications that lie hidden beneath the surface.

Like many saints and sinners, More had such a vision. The key to understanding how they viewed life and death lies in the exhortation he wrote in a letter to loved ones just before he died: "Be merry in God!"

Be merry—but be merry *in God*. Without God—without the hope of another world beyond this one, for which this one is longing—there could be no true merriment. There could be only the shallow giggle of flippancy or the hollow mockery of the cynic. To be truly merry is to live lightly in this world, to be unburdened with cares about things that are quickly passing away.

Perhaps, then, a part of what it means to be, as Jesus said, *in* the world but not *of* the world (see John 17:15–18) is to be laughing *at* the world. We might say that for those who take God and his will with appropriate seriousness, nothing else need be taken seriously, even death—especially death.

No wonder Saint Thomas More and many others, enduring the ordinary trials we all suffer and a few extraordinary ones besides, remained merry for a lifetime and into their final hours. In their living and in their dying they fulfilled Jesus' prophecy: "You have pain now; but...your hearts will rejoice, and no one will take your joy from you."

* * *

Saint Lawrence (d. 258), a Spanish-born deacon of Rome, suffered martyrdom during Emperor Valerian's persecution. When the Roman prefect had him bound to a red-hot griddle, he endured the torment with extraordinary grace, saying at one point to his executioners: "My flesh is well-cooked on this one side. Turn the other, and eat."

François Rabelais (c. 1494–1553) was a Franciscan novice, then a Benedictine monk, physician and writer noted for humor and satire. His last will and testament said: "I have no available property; I owe a great deal; the rest I leave to the poor."

Oscar Wilde (1854–1900) was the witty and controversial Irish-born author and playwright known best in England and America for such comedies as *The Importance of Being Earnest*. Toward the end of his life he became Catholic, after having served prison time for breaking British anti-sodomy laws. Noting that the twentieth century was about to begin, he remarked, sipping champagne on his deathbed: "It would really be more than the English could stand if another century began and I were still alive. I am dying, as I have lived...beyond my means." He reportedly also said, looking at the walls: "I am in a duel to death with this wallpaper. One of us has to go."

Anne Boleyn (c. 1501–1536), second wife of King Henry VIII, remarked on the night before she was beheaded: "The people will have no difficulty finding a nickname for me. I shall be Queen Anne Lackhead."

Brendan Behan (1923–1964), the Irish playwright, poet and novelist, said to his wife just before he died from alcohol- and diabetes-related complications: "You made one mistake. You married me." Later he said to the nun who was wiping his feverish forehead: "May all your sons be bishops."

John Barrymore (1882–1942), an American actor from a family of famous actors, declared during his final illness: "Die? I should say not, my dear fellow. No Barrymore would ever allow such a conventional thing to happen to him."

Saint John Bosco often joked during the prolonged illness that ended in his death. One day he asked the boys: "Don't any of you know of a bellows factory?"

Puzzled, they asked, "But why?"

"Why?" he replied. "To place an order for two new lungs. Mine are not worth a cent between them."

Hillaire Belloc (1870–1953), the British author and apologist known for his caustic wit, died from burns received in an accident at home. As he was dying he cracked: "Better burn the writer than his work!"

The epitaph he wrote for himself was never used on his tombstone: "His sins were scarlet, but his books were read."

Saint Thomas More jested to the sergeant-at-arms as he made his way up the wobbly stairs of the scaffold: "See me safe up. For my coming down I can shift for myself."

To the executioner he said: "Courage, my good man; don't be afraid. But take care, for I have a short neck, and you must look to your honor."

Finally, as the martyr laid his head on the chopping block, he carefully moved his beard out of the path of the ax, commenting: "It does not deserve to be cut off, since it has betrayed nothing!"

James Michael Curley (1874–1958) was mayor of Boston and governor of Massachusetts, a colorful political boss. As he was wheeled off a hospital elevator after surgery, he insisted: "I wish to announce the first plank in my campaign for reelection. We're going to have the floors in this *&%$! hospital smoothed out!"

Jeane-François Ducos (1765–1793) was a leader in the French Revolution who was guillotined in the Reign of Terror. He joked on the scaffold: "The Convention has forgotten one decree: a decree on the indivisibility of heads and bodies."

Lodovico Cortusio (d. 1418), an Italian nobleman, forbade anyone to mourn openly at his funeral. Anyone discovered weeping would be disinherited, but the one who laughed most heartily would be his principal heir and universal legatee. His will called specifically for "the sound of lutes, violins, oboes, trumpets, tambourines and other musical instruments." His funeral was reportedly a great celebration.

Francisco Franco (1892–1975), Spanish soldier and dictator, was told as he lay dying that General Garcia wished to say good-bye to him. He replied: "Why? Is Garcia going on a trip?"

Pietro Aretino (1492–1556) was an Italian satirist, nicknamed "the Scourge of Princes." After receiving the oil of extreme unction, he reportedly said: "Keep rats away, now that I'm all greased up."

Alfred Hitchcock (1899–1980), a movie and television director known as the master of suspense, was a devout Catholic. He remarked near the end: "One has to die to know exactly what happens after death, although Catholics have their hopes."

Elisabeth Patterson Bonaparte (1785–1869) was an American-born socialite who married the youngest brother of the French emperor Napoleon. Someone in the room where she was dying noted that nothing was so certain as death. She added: "Except taxes."

Richard I engaged in lighthearted banter with a monk as he was dying. The monk urged him to think of his three daughters. When the Lion Heart protested that he had no daughters, the monk insisted that indeed he did, and they were named Pride, Avarice and Lust.

"Well, then," replied the king, "I'll marry them off: the first to the [Knights] Templar, the second to the Grey [Tironensian monks] and the third to the Black [Benedictine] Monks."

Joel Chandler Harris (1848–1908) was the American journalist and storyteller who collected and edited the Uncle Remus stories from former slaves in coastal Georgia and South Carolina. Married to a Catholic, he entered the church himself only a few weeks before his death. Asked as he lay sick whether he felt any better, he replied: "I feel about the extent of a tenth of a gnat's eyebrow better."

Joseph Lieutaud (1703–1780), medical researcher and physician to the French king, replied to colleagues proposing various remedies for his illness: "Ah, I shall die well enough without all that!"

Voltaire (1694–1778), the French Enlightenment author and skeptic, has had attributed to him a humorously cynical remark that is likely apocryphal—since at least six irreligious historical figures are reported to have made the same statement before they died. According to the story, when a priest asked him on his deathbed to renounce Satan, he replied: "Now, my good man, this is no time for making enemies."

Stanislaw I (1677–1766), king of Poland, died from burns received when his bathrobe caught fire. Of the robe he quipped: "You gave it to me to warm me, but it has kept me too hot!"

Charles Maurice de Talleyrand (1754–1838), the French statesman, was told on his deathbed: "The archbishop of Paris would willingly give his life for you." He replied:

"He can find a much better use for it."

Alexandre Dumas the elder, suffering from the effects of a stroke, showed his son two coins and said: "Everybody has said that I was a prodigal. You yourself wrote a play about it. And so, do you see how you were mistaken? When I first landed in Paris, I had two [coins] in my pocket. Look! I still have them!"

Henry John (Jackie) Gleason (1916–1987), the popular American actor and comedian, said shortly before he died: "If God wants another joke man, I'm ready."

James Joyce (1882–1941), the Irish author perhaps best known for his novel *Ulysses,* on regaining consciousness after surgery was told that he had received blood donated by two soldiers from Neuchâtel, Switzerland. He responded: "A good omen. I like Neuchâtel wine."

Louis XII (1462–1515), king of France, died on New Year's Day, less than three months after marrying the teenage sister of King Henry VIII of England, who despised him. He told her: "Darling, as a New Year's present, I give you my death."

Francis Joseph (Frank) Sheed (1897–1981) was an Australian lawyer and theological writer who, with his British wife, Maisie Ward, founded the Catholic publishing company Sheed & Ward. Refusing an unappetizing meal from the hospital cafeteria, he quipped: "I fancy I'll let it live."

Henri Toulouse-Lautrec (1864–1901), a French painter, illustrator and lithographer, said to the priest who came to visit him on his deathbed: "I am happier to see you now than I shall be in a few days, when you come with your little bell."

Saint Mary Mazzarello (1837–1881) was the Italian cofounder, with Saint John Bosco, of the Salesian sisters. When she had received last rites, she asked the priest: "Father, now that I have my passport, have I permission to leave?"

Saint Mathias Mulumba (d. 1886) was an African chief and one of the Martyrs of Uganda, dismembered and exposed to the elements to die several days later. Dragged before the prime minister, he was condemned to death for actions unworthy of a chief, among them, "doing his own cooking." Mathias replied with a smile: "Am I on trial for my thinness or my religion?"

Saint Louis Orione was sent to an infirmary to recover from two strokes. He joked with the infirmarian about his sickroom, whose only light was a small votive candle before a picture of our Lady: "Don't you think that this place is exactly like a mortuary chapel?"

Alexander Pope (1688–1744), the English poet and satirist, was encouraged by his doctor to take heart in the fact that he displayed a few good physical symptoms. "I am dying, Sir," he replied, "of one hundred good symptoms."

John Philpot Curran (1750–1817), an Irish author, politician and wit, was told by his doctor that he was coughing "with more difficulty." He responded: "That is surprising, since I have been practicing all night."

Bob Hope (1903–2003), the popular American actor and comedian, was asked as he was dying where he wanted to be buried. He replied: "Surprise me."

Wilson Mizner (1876–1933) was an American con artist, dramatist and wit. On his deathbed he regained consciousness momentarily to discover a priest beside the bed. "Why should I talk to you?" he asked him. "I've just been talking to your boss!"

Comtesse de Vercillis (d. 1728) was a French noblewoman whose death was later described by a friend, the philosopher Jean Jacques Rousseau. After breaking wind she said to an embarrassed visitor: "Good! A woman who can fart is not dead!"

ELEVEN

"Into Your Hands"
GOD'S WORD IN THEIR MOUTHS

> *Then Jesus, crying with a*
> *loud voice, said, "Father,*
> *into your hands I*
> *commend my spirit."*
> *Having said this, he*
> *breathed his last.*
> —Luke 23:46

WHEN HURRICANE KATRINA LEFT THE CITY OF NEW Orleans in ruins, those who watched the tragedy unfold before the network television cameras were aghast at the sight: Stranded residents and tourists found themselves surrounded not just by rising floodwaters but by hunger and thirst, crime and confusion, darkness and death.

In the midst of that horror, one desperate woman took her stand outside the city's convention center, where thousands of survivors were waiting for rescue, and began to pray. At the top of her lungs, she shouted: "The Lord is my shepherd, I shall not want!" (Psalm 23:1). Others nearby joined in, reciting the rest of the familiar psalm, whose words have brought comfort to believers for thousands of years.

When terrors surround us, what better refuge can we find than sacred Scripture? In its words we hear the powerful, consoling voice of God. Our faith is strengthened and our fears subdued.

Jesus knew Scripture intimately; it was woven into the fabric of his thought and speech. He cited it often in his teaching, and as we have already seen, when he faced his darkest hour, he made its words his own. Not only his anguished cry from the cross, "Why have you forsaken me?" but also his last prayer before dying, "Into your hands I commend my spirit," came from the Psalms (Matthew 27:46; Psalm 22:1; Luke 23:46; Psalm 31:5).

Ever since that first Good Friday, Catholics have imitated their Lord by taking the word of God into their mouths at the moment of death. Many have repeated Jesus' quote from Psalm 31, "Into your hands I commend my spirit": Saint Thomas the apostle, Saint Mark the evangelist, Saint Nicholas, Charlemagne, Saint Catherine of Siena, Saint Bridget of Sweden, Henry V, Christopher Columbus, Saint John of the Cross, Saint Aloysius Gonzaga and Blessed Pope John XXIII, among others.

Psalm 31 also contains the prayer "In you, O Lord, I seek refuge; do not let me be put to shame." A number of Catholics have used these words to express their firm trust in God in the hour of death, including bishop and martyr John Fisher (who prayed this prayer on the scaffold), France's "terrible king" Louis XI and Saint Hyacinth of Poland.

For some the word of God becomes, as it did for Jesus, a final prayer to the Father. For others it provides an apt summary of the lives they are offering. For still others it is a final profession of faith, cry for mercy or expression of hope in the life to come.

In each of these situations, the dying are binding themselves not only to God but to believers everywhere, in generations past and generations to come, who have lived and died feeding on the sacred texts. However varied their life stories may have been, at the end they all converged, joining in a single chorus that chants God's word in unison.

The same is true for those who died repeating the solemn prayers and professions of the church. These prayers are founded in Scripture and have sprung from it like so many luxurious branches: the creeds, the Our Father, the rosary, the Divine Office, the *Anima Christi*, the Act of Resignation and others. Above all, the church's prayers for the dying have remained a matchless source of comfort and strength at the hour of death.

Yet there is another sense in which we Catholics may take the Word of God into our mouths as we are dying. For "the Word became flesh and lived among us" (John 1:14). Christ himself is the Word of God, and he gives himself wholly to us in the Eucharist. For that reason the holy *viaticum* (in Latin, literally "food for the journey" from this world to the next) is the church's last, best gift to the dying: a final Communion on earth with the very Body and Blood, Soul and Divinity of the Savior.

In this sacrament and in the others that we may be privileged to receive before death—reconciliation and anointing of the sick—divine grace meets us and ushers us across the threshold into eternity.

***

Heinrich der Loewe (c. 1129–1195), called Henry the Lion, was the former duke of Saxony and Bavaria. He quoted the prayer of the penitent tax collector in Jesus' parable (Luke 18:13): "God, be merciful to me, a sinner."

Jean de Gerson (1363–1429) was a French theologian and mystic and the chancellor of the University of Paris. His last words included the Canticle of Simeon, known in Latin as the *Nunc Dimittis*: "Now, O Lord, let your servant depart in peace" (Luke 2:29).

François-Joseph le Clerc du Tremblay (1577–1638) was a Capuchin priest and adviser to Richelieu known as Father Joseph. His last words echoed the warning from the Book of Hebrews for spiritual leaders: "Render an account; render an account" (Hebrews 13:17).

Saint Francis Xavier (1506–1552), the Spanish Jesuit missionary to the Far East, was known as the "Apostle of the Indies" and the "Apostle of Japan." He died repeating the words of the blind man who begged Jesus to heal him: "Jesus, Son of David, have mercy on me!" (Mark 10:47).

Saint Babylas (d. 251), bishop of Antioch and martyr, quoted Psalm 116:7: "Return, O my soul, to your rest, for the LORD has dealt bountifully with you."

Saint Getulius (d. 124) was a wealthy Roman catechist and the host of a house church. When ordered by Roman imperial officials to sacrifice to Jupiter and Mars or die, he replied: "I thank my God, the Father Almighty, that I am able to offer him an acceptable sacrifice."

He was asked, "What sacrifice?"

His reply echoed Psalm 51:17: "The sacrifice of a broken and contrite heart."

Saint Teresa of Jesus (Avila) quoted the same verse just a few moments before she died: "A sacrifice to God is an afflicted spirit. ... A humble and contrite heart, O God, you will not despise."

Saint Peter of Alcantara (1499–1562), a Spanish Franciscan mystical writer, recited Psalm 122:1: "I was glad when they said to me, 'Let us go to the house of the Lord!'"

Pope Paul III (1468–1549), who convened the Council of Trent, recited Psalm 19:13 (Vulgate) as he died: "Keep back your servant also from presumptuous sins; do not let them have dominion over me! Then I shall be blameless, and innocent of great transgression."

Pope Saint Gregory VII (1020–1085) fought attempts by secular rulers to control the church. He was finally exiled by the Holy Roman Emperor Henry IV. Paraphrasing Psalm 45:7, he lamented: "I have loved justice and hated iniquity. Therefore I die in exile."

Cornelia Connelly (1809–1879), an American Catholic convert and founder of the Society of the Holy Child of Jesus, echoed the words of Job 19:26, affirming her faith in the resurrection of the body: "In this flesh I shall see my God!"

Blessed Brother André Bessette said a few days before his death at age ninety-one: "The great Almighty is coming."

Just moments before his death, rousing from a coma, he whispered: "Here is the grain." Perhaps he had in mind Jesus' words: "Unless a grain of wheat falls into the earth and dies, it remains just a single grain; but if it dies, it bears much fruit" (John 12:24).

Oscar Arnulfo Romero (1917–1980) was archbishop of San Salvador, the capital of El Salvador. He openly demanded justice and peace from the national government, a military regime characterized by oppressive violence and violation of human rights. Just before his murder by a gunman under orders from the military, he was preaching at Mass about Jesus' description of the grain of wheat that must die:

> Those who surrender to the service of the poor through the love of Christ will live like the grain of wheat that dies. It only apparently dies. If it were not to die, it would remain a solitary grain. The harvest comes because of the grain that dies. We know that every effort to improve society, above all when society is so full of injustice and sin, is an effort that God blesses, that God wants, that God demands of us.

Saint Bede (c. 673–735), the Anglo-Saxon scholar, historian and theologian, was anxious to finish his translation of the Gospel of Saint John, knowing that he had only moments to live. He said to the scribe, "Write quickly!" Then he addressed Christ, referring to the words from the cross that he had just translated: "Well, you have spoken truly: 'It is finished.' ... Glory be to the Father, and to the Son, and to the Holy Spirit!"

Saint Louis IX (1214–1270), king of France, celebrated for his justice and personal piety, died of the plague on a crusade in North Africa. He asked to be laid on a bed covered with ashes as an act of penance; then he crossed his arms upon his chest and looked toward heaven, praying a paraphrase of Psalm 5:7: "I will enter into your temple! I will adore you in your holy house! I will confess your name!"

Pope Saint Pius X spoke his last words to his doctor, referring to Saint Paul's word to the Ephesians (1:9–10): "Together in one—all things in Christ."

Saint Bernard of Clairveaux His last words to his monks echoed Saint Paul's words to the Philippians at the end of his life (see Philippians 1:23–24): "I am in a strait between two things: having a desire to depart and be with Christ, and yet to stay with you."

Roger B. Taney (1777–1864), the American jurist who was the first Catholic to become chief justice of the United States Supreme Court, quoted the dying prayer of Saint Stephen, the first martyr, from the Book of Acts (7:59): "Lord Jesus, receive my spirit!"

Saint Francis of Assisi died, as he had lived, singing. He chanted Psalm 142: *"Voce mea ad Dominum clamavi,"* "With my voice I cry to the Lord."

Paul-Thérèse-David d'Astros (1772–1851), the French cardinal archbishop of Toulouse, died referring to Saint Paul's words to the Romans (8:38–39): "Neither life nor death nor any being can separate us from him."

Saint Augustine of Hippo (354–430), bishop, theologian and doctor of the church, quoted Christ's words in Gethsemane (see Matthew 26:42), adding the final call for Christ to return in the Book of Revelation (Revelation 22:20): "Your will be done. Come, Lord Jesus!"

Pope Paul VI (1897–1978) reigned during the final years of the Second Vatican Council. As the Nicene Creed was recited at his bedside, he repeated the phrase "apostolic church, apostolic church." After receiving the Eucharist, he prayed softly the prayer our Savior taught us: "Our Father, who art in heaven...."

Pope Pius XII (1876–1958) fell asleep saying the rosary but awoke again and insisted: "I must finish the rosary I began."

Saint Elizabeth Ann Bayley Seton (1774–1821), foundress of the American Sisters of Charity, was the first native-born American to be canonized. Dying of tuberculosis, she prayed the traditional Act of Resignation to the Will of God: "May the most just, the most high, and the most amiable will of God be in all things fulfilled, praised, and exalted above all forevermore!"

Soon afterward she prayed the final words of the traditional *Anima Christi* prayer: "At the hour of death, call me and bid me come to you, that with your saints I may praise you forever and ever!"

At the end she said simply, "Jesus."

Saint Dominic de Guzmán joined those around him in the traditional prayers for the dying: "Come to my aid, saints of God, and bear my soul into the presence of the Most High."

Pope Pius IX (1792–1878) was surrounded by people praying the *Proficere,* which begins, "Go forth, Christian soul." He whispered: "Yes, go forth. ... Yes, go forth."

Jean-François de Laharpe (1739–1803) was a French poet and literary critic. He told the priest administering the last rites: "I am grateful to Divine Mercy for having left me sufficient recollection to feel how consoling these prayers are to the dying."

Saint Francis Solano (1549–1610), called the "Wonder Worker of the New World," was a Spanish Franciscan priest and missionary to South America. Priests and friars surrounded his deathbed and recited the Apostles' Creed. When they came to the words "he was conceived by the Holy Spirit, born of the Virgin Mary," Francis suddenly threw his arms out in the form of a cross, crying triumphantly: "God be praised!"

Saint Edmund Campion (c. 1540–1581), an English Jesuit, was tortured, hanged, drawn and quartered in the persecution of Catholics by Queen Elizabeth I. At his execution he responded to a Protestant minister's exhortation to pray in English: "Do you mind? I will pray to God in a language that we both well understand." Then he continued praying traditional Latin prayers of the church.

Saint Anthony of Padua (c. 1190–1231) was a Portuguese Franciscan priest, preacher and doctor of the church. As he was dying he recited the penitential psalms and then the Lauds hymn *O Gloriosa Domina* ("O Glorious Lady"), ending with the words "Assist us at the hour of our death."

Charles Carroll (1737–1832), the American revolutionary statesman and ambassador, was the only Catholic signer of the Declaration of Independence and the last of the signers to die. To his physician, who pressed him to eat, he said: "Thank you, Doctor, not just now. This ceremony [of last rites] is so deeply interesting to the Christian that it supplies all the wants of nature. I have no more desire for food."

Saint Camillus de Lellis cried out as the priest administering last rites sprinkled the holy water only sparingly: "More water! More holy water!" When the priest complied, he commented: "Now that is all right."

Louis XV (1710–1774), king of France, died of smallpox after reigning fifty-nine years. When the last rites had been administered, he said: "I have never felt better, or more at peace."

Jules Verne (1828–1905), the French science fiction writer, on his deathbed said to his family: "Good! You're all there. Now I can die." When the priest finished administering the last rites, he said to him: "You have done me good. I feel regenerated."

Ludwig van Beethoven (1770–1827), the celebrated German composer, is the subject of conflicting accounts about how he met his death. In one version he received the last rites and then said to his priest: "I thank you, Reverend Sir. You have brought me comfort."

Pietro Metastasio (1698–1782), an Italian poet and operatic librettist, prayed after receiving the Eucharist in the last rites: "I offer you, O Lord, your own Son, who has already given me a pledge of love enclosed in this thin Emblem. Turn your eyes on him. Ah, behold Whom I offer you, and then desist, O Lord, if you can from mercy!"

Saint Jean-Marie-Baptiste Vianney (1786–1859), as the Eucharist was brought to him for the last time, exclaimed: "How kind the good God is! When we are no longer able to go to him, he himself comes to us!"

Then tears came to his eyes. He was asked, "Father, why do you weep? In just a little while you'll be in heaven."

He replied: "Yes, but it is sad to receive Holy Communion for the last time."

Leon Adelard Fafard (d. 1885) was a priest ministering in the settlement of Frog Lake, Northwest Territories of Canada, when the Minnesota Sioux Uprising took place. Big Bear's Cree warriors captured the settlement; the result was the Frog Lake Massacre. Just moments before being killed, Father Fafard rushed to a fallen man and administered the last rites. His final words offered assurance to that dying friend: "My poor brother, I think you are safe with God."

TWELVE

"Keep My Commandments"
W I S D O M

> *If you keep my*
> *commandments, you will*
> *abide in my love, just as I*
> *have kept my Father's*
> *commandments and abide*
> *in his love.*
> —John 15:10

"GET WISDOM," URGED THAT WISEST OF ANCIENT MEN,
King Solomon. "Prize her highly, and she will exalt you;
she will honor you if you embrace her" (Proverbs 4:7, 8).

Wisdom is often death's companion. She comes to
invite the dying to one last embrace. Those who realize that
their days are numbered know themselves to be dust; and in
that sobering knowledge, as the psalmist observed, they
"gain a wise heart" (Psalm 90:12). They may also find that
death's approach distills the precious lessons of a lifetime.

Not surprisingly, the dying often feel compelled to
pass on whatever wisdom they have achieved. Recognized
leaders may provide their followers with explicit instructions or even commands, as Jesus did in long exhortations
the night he was betrayed. Some of the most cherished of
Scripture verses, crystallizing beautifully the essential
truths of the gospel, come to us from Saint John's record
of these final directives (see John 13:1–17:26).

Even people of much less authority—moral, spiritual or otherwise—make their own contributions to the world's treasury of wisdom. Consider, for example, the rough-edged sagacity of the French entertainer Edith Piaf. Her warning to her sister, at the end of a rather colorful life, was simple: "All the damned-fool things you do in life, you pay for."

Sometimes the wisdom comes to us like a tiny pearl: smooth, simple and unfaceted, but a gem nonetheless. For the Italian religious sister Teresa Valse Pantellini, it was the maxim that we should be "resolved to pass unnoticed." For the Italian composer Giacomo Puccini, it was a last remark to his stepdaughter: "Remember that your mother is a remarkable woman."

In all these insights from the dying, we find, at least implicitly, echoes of our Lord's final command to "abide in love."

* * *

Saint Achard (c. 1100–1172), the English-born bishop of Avranches and abbot of Saint Victor, Paris, instructed his monks: "What I enjoin above all, the one thing needful, is to take care lest the author of evil sow hatred among you and break the peace of the [community]. You are not unaware that hatred [separates us] from God and closes heaven to [us]. No suffering can expiate hate; it is not redeemed by martyrdom; it is a stain that all the blood in us would fail to wash."

G.K. Chesterton (1874–1936), the British journalist, fiction writer and Catholic apologist, declared: "The issue is now clear. It is between light and darkness, and everyone must choose his side."

Saint Louis IX was celebrated for his justice and personal piety. Dying of the plague on a crusade in North Africa, he prayed: "O Lord God, grant that we may so despise the prosperity of this world that we stand in no fear of adversity."

Charles Carroll said to his priest shortly before he died: "I have lived to my ninety-sixth year. I have enjoyed continued health. I have been blessed with great wealth, prosperity and most of the good things that the world can bestow—public approbation, esteem, applause. But what I now look back on with greatest satisfaction to myself is that I have practiced the duties of my religion."

Pope Clement XI (1649–1721) reigned more than twenty years. He advised his nephew, a cardinal: "See how all the honors of the world come to an end. Only that is great which is great in God's sight. Make it your endeavor to be a saint."

Blessed Charles de Foucauld (1858–1916), a French-born priest, missionary to the nomadic Taureg people of Morocco and founder of the Union of Brothers and Sisters of the Sacred Heart, was murdered by local insurrectionists. He had written in a letter on the morning of the day he died: "When we are reduced to nothing, it is the most powerful means we have to unite ourselves with Jesus and to do good to souls."

Dante Alighieri (1265–1321), the Italian poet and philosopher best known for his *Divine Comedy,* was asked for political advice. He replied: "You ask too much of me. Dedicate your strength and your spirit to your prince and your country, and leave to God the mysterious balance of fortune. Every banner that is not borne by a traitor leads to virtue."

Saint Cuthbert (c. 634–687), an English bishop and abbot, said to his monks: "Know and remember, that if of two evils you are compelled to choose one, I would rather that you should take my bones and leave these places, to reside wherever God may send you, than consent in any way to the wickedness of schismatics, and so place a yoke upon your necks."

Karl Theodor von Dalberg (1744–1817), a German noble who was the last archbishop-elector of Mainz, proposed a final toast: "Love! Life! ... To God's will!"

Saint John the Abbot (fourth century), told his monks: "Never have I done my own will, and never have I taught others to do what I had not first done myself!"

Lorenzo de' Medici advised: "Pursue the line of conduct marked out by the strictest integrity, as regards the interests of the whole, not the wishes of a part of the community."

Saint John Bosco told the poor and neglected boys he had served: "Live together as brothers, love each other and bear with each other. The protection of Our Lady, Help of Christians, will always be with you."

A few days later he gave his last instructions: "Frequent Communion and devotion to our Lady will be their safeguard."

Charles Nerinckx (1761–1824) was a Belgian missionary to America known as the "Apostle of Kentucky." He founded the Sisters of Loretto at the Foot of the Cross. Dying at a mission outpost in what is now Missouri, he left in his will these instructions for the sisters:

"Zeal for souls—your own and that of so many desolate orphans and scholars—burning zeal of Jesus and Mary! Gain souls, hunt souls, catch souls, court souls, draw souls, pull souls, carry souls, deliver souls, shelter souls, buy souls! ... Souls! Souls! And nothing but souls, for the love of Jesus, the owner of all souls!"

Philip II (1527–1598), king of Spain, whose ulcer-ridden body crawled with worms and bore an intolerable stench, declared to his son and successor:

> I meant to save you this scene, but I wish you to see how the monarchies of the earth end. You see that God has [stripped] me of all the glory and majesty of a monarch in order to hand them to you. In a few hours I shall be covered only with a poor shroud and girded with a coarse rope. The king's crown is already falling from my brow, and death will place it upon yours.
>
> Two things I especially commend to you: one is that you always keep faithful to the holy Catholic church, and the other is that you treat your subjects justly. The crown will one day fall from your head as it now falls from mine. You are young, as I once was. My days are numbered and draw to a close. The tale of yours God alone knows, but they too must end.

Michelangelo Buonarroti (1475–1564), the celebrated Italian sculptor, painter, architect and poet, wrote in his last will and testament: "I commit my soul to the hands of God, my body to the earth and my substance to my nearest relatives, enjoining upon these last, when their hour comes, to think upon the sufferings of Jesus Christ."

Pierre-Paul Royer-Collard (1763–1845) was a French philosopher and politician who openly opposed the anti-Catholic tendencies of the French Revolution. His last words: "There is nothing substantial in the world but religious ideas. Never give them up, or if you do, come back to them."

Alfred the Great (c. 849–899), king of the West Saxons, said to his son and successor:

> We must now part. I go to another world, and you are to be left alone in possession of all that I have thus far held. I beg you, dear child, to be a father to your people. Be the children's father and the widow's friend. Comfort the poor, protect and shelter the weak, and with all your might, right that which is wrong.
>
> And, my son, govern yourself by law. Then shall the Lord love you, and God himself shall be your reward. Call upon him to advise you in all your need, and he shall help you to fulfill all your desires.

Alexander Pope said at the end: "There is nothing that is meritorious but virtue and friendship, and indeed friendship itself is only a part of virtue."

Blessed André Bessette said: "How good God is! How powerful! How beautiful! He must indeed be so beautiful, since the soul, which is but a ray of his beauty, is so lovely!"

Jean-Baptiste Dubos (1670–1742), a French historian and diplomat, said of his approaching demise: "Death is a law and not a punishment. Three things ought to console us for giving up life: the friends whom we have lost, the few persons worthy of being loved whom we leave behind us and finally the memory of our stupidities and the assurance that they are now going to stop."

Bertrand du Guesclin (c. 1320–1380), a French military leader and constable of France, told the military men gathered around his deathbed: "Remember that your business is only with those who carry arms. The churchmen, the poor, the women and children are not your enemies. ... Farewell; I am at an end."

Pope Eugene IV (1383–1447) advised on his deathbed: "Pray only that God will perform his will. I have often begged in my prayers for what would have been better not to have prayed."

Saint Gilbert of Sempringham (1085–1189) was the founder of the Gilbertian Order in England. To the religious of his order, he said: "Three maxims I have always tried to observe I now commend to you: first, never to hurt anyone, and, if injured, never to seek revenge; secondly, to bear patiently whatever suffering God may inflict, remembering that 'he chastens everyone whom he receives' [Hebrews 12:6]; and finally, to obey those in authority so as not to be a stumbling block for others."

Louis VI the Fat (1081–1137), king of France, spoke these parting words to his son: "Remember, my son, that kingship is a public charge, for which you will have to render a strict account in another world."

Saint Hilda (614–680) was an English noblewoman who became an abbess renowned for her spiritual wisdom. Her final instructions to her nuns were "Handmaids of Christ, maintain the peace of the gospel with each other and with all."

Louis XIV almost bankrupted France through costly wars. Dying of diabetes, he said to his little great-grandson, heir to the throne:

> Sweet child, you are about to be a great king, but your whole happiness will depend on your submission to God, and on the care you take to relieve the people of their burden. In order to do this you must, whenever you can, avoid making war: it is the ruin of the people.
>
> Do not follow the bad example I have given you on this point. Often I have started wars without sufficient cause and continued them to satisfy my pride. Do not imitate me. Be a peaceful ruler, and let your main object be to look after your subjects.

Thomas Moore (1779–1852), the Irish Romantic poet, outlived all his children. When his time came to die, his wife was distraught over being left alone. He told her: "Lean upon God, Bessie; lean upon God."

Pope Saint Sylvester I (c. 270–335) urged his priests as he was dying: "Love one another, govern your churches diligently and protect your flocks from the teeth of wolves."

Saint Thomas Aquinas was asked, "What is the best way to live without offending God?" He replied, just before his last breath: "He who walks in the presence of God and is always ready to give an account of his actions to him certainly will never be separated from him by sin."

Wiera Francia (1898–1929), an Italian teacher, Carmelite tertiary and local leader in Catholic Action, died from a perforate intestine. After receiving the last rites, she wrote the final entry in her diary:

> Your sanctification is the first activity to which Jesus wishes you to apply yourself....If you wish to become holy, you must not think of beginning next month, or tomorrow or even in an hour. You must begin this very instant. Only if you divide up your activities in this way—hour by hour, minute by minute—will you be able to apply yourself with effectiveness, because it is just in this way that Jesus gives you His grace. Think of being a saint today and begin this very hour, or rather this minute, and afterward let Jesus act.

Conrad Hilton (1887–1979) wrote in his last will and testament to the directors and trustees of the charitable foundation he set up:

> There is a natural law, a Divine law, that obliges you and me to relieve the suffering, the distressed and the destitute. Charity is a supreme virtue, and the great channel through which the mercy of God is passed on to mankind. It is the virtue that unites men and inspires their noblest efforts.
>
> "Love one another, for that is the whole law"; so our fellowmen deserve to be loved and encouraged—never to be abandoned to walk alone in poverty and darkness. The practice of charity will bind us—will bind all men in one great brotherhood.

THIRTEEN

"Here Is Your Mother"
CONCERN FOR THOSE LEFT BEHIND

> *Then he said to the
> disciple, "Here is your
> mother." And from that
> hour the disciple took her
> into his own home.*
> —John 19:27

SHE STANDS IN THE SHADOW OF THE CROSS, WEEPING,
watching, waiting for the end. Each time her Son groans,
his pain pierces her through. She suffers every agony with
him, though her suffering is of a different kind—the kind
that only a parent could understand.

Jesus turns his head toward her, and the sight of her
adds yet another grief to his already infinite burden. She
has grown old, and Joseph is long gone. She has no other
children. After all that has happened, her old friends and
neighbors are afraid to be seen with her. Who will care for
her now?

From the depths of his anguish Jesus summons the
strength to clear his mind and resolve the matter: he himself will find his mother another son. Though one of the
Twelve betrayed him, and ten more of them are in hiding,
John has taken his place beside her; John it will be.

"Here is your mother," he tells the Beloved Apostle. Jesus is entrusting to him the one on earth he has loved most. The young man understands, and from that day forward Mary has a new home.

In some ways this is the most poignant scene from Jesus' hours on the cross. When he had every reason to be focused on himself and his plight, his concern instead was for someone he would leave behind.

And so it has been for many of his followers. In their dying words they turned their attention to those for whom they had a special bond of fondness or responsibility. Parents thought of their children; sovereigns, their subjects; teachers, their disciples; pastors, their flock.

Some expressed their care and concern through a grand gesture: Pope Benedict XV, who had seen great carnage in World War I, prayed: "I willingly offer my life for the peace of the world." On a much more modest scale, but touching in its own way, is Queen Marie Antoinette's apology to her executioner when she stepped on his foot on their way to the scaffold: "I beg your pardon, Sir. I didn't do it on purpose."

If these and so many more could think of others first even as they were dying, surely we who are left behind can do the same in our daily lives.

* * *

Lili Boulanger (1893–1918), a French composer, died after years of suffering. She said at the end to her family: "I offer to God my sufferings so that they may shower down on you as joys."

Henry II (1519–1559), king of France, whose reign was largely spent in wars with surrounding kingdoms, was fatally injured in a tournament. He told his son, heir to the throne: "My boy, you are going to be without your father, but not without his blessing. I pray that God will make you more fortunate than I have been."

Philippa of Hainault (1314–1369), queen consort of Edward III, king of England, told her husband: "My husband, we have enjoyed our long union in happiness, peace and prosperity. I entreat, before I depart and we are forever separated in this world, that you grant me three requests: the payment of my lawful debts, the fulfillment of the legacies of my will and my wish that you be buried beside me in the cloisters of Westminster when your time comes."

Saint Antony the Great (251–356) was the ancient Egyptian abbot known as the "Father of Monasticism." His farewell instructions to his monks: "Distribute my garments thus: To Athanasius, the bishop, give one of my sheepskins and the cloak under me, which was new when he gave it to me and has grown old by [my use of it]; and to Serapion, the bishop, give the other sheepskin; and [you are to] have the haircloth garment. And for the rest, children, farewell, for Antony is going and is with you no more."

Padre Pio, just before he died, said to his grandnephew named Pio: "You carry my name. I want you to live up to it. Understand?"

Saint John Bosco, near the end of a long illness, told his boys: "The only sacrifice I shall have to make is leaving you." His last words referred to the boys: "Tell them that I shall wait for them all in paradise."

Saint Martin of Tours announced to his disciples that he was dying, and they cried out: "Don't leave us!" Martin wept and responded not to them but to God:

> Lord, if I am still necessary to my people, I do not refuse the labor.
>
> Lord, the battles one must fight in the flesh for your service are hard, and I have already fought battles enough. But if you command me to labor on, to mount guard before your camp, I do not refuse or plead the exhaustion of age. I shall devote myself to whatever task you may still lay upon me. If it is your will to consider my great age, your will is all the good I need. As for the flock for whom I fear, you know how to guard it.

Eva Braun Hitler (1912–1945) was Adolf Hitler's mistress and finally his wife. Just before entering a bunker beneath Berlin to commit suicide with her husband, she said to one of the secretaries: "Take my fur coat. I've always liked well-dressed people."

Robert Tyre (Bobby) Jones (1902–1971), the golfing champion from Georgia, converted to the Catholic faith on his deathbed to please his wife. He told his priest: "You know, if I had known how happy this had made Mary, I would have done it years ago."

Alfred the Great said to his son: "I desire to leave to the men that come after me a remembrance of me in good works."

Baron Georges Cuvier (1769–1832) was a French naturalist. As he was dying he passed on a glass of lemonade to his daughter-in-law, remarking: "It is very delightful to see those I love still able to swallow."

Léon-Michel de Gambetta (1838–1882) was a French statesman. Awakened by a friend's falling in a faint upon hearing that Gambetta's illness would be fatal, he exclaimed: "Good heavens! Has he hurt himself?"

Blessed Kateri Tekakwitha (c. 1656–1680), an Algonquin consecrated virgin, lived among the Mohawks in what is now New York. She said to a loved one:

> I am leaving you. I am going to die. Remember always what we have done together since we first met. If you change I shall accuse you before the tribunal of God.
>
> Take courage. Despise the discoursings of those who have not the faith. If they ever try to persuade you to marry, listen only to the [Jesuit] fathers. If you cannot

serve God here, go to the mission at Lorette. Don't give up your mortifications.

I shall love you in heaven. I shall pray for you. I shall aid you....

Jesus, I love you! Jesus! Mary!

Frédéric Chopin said to two friends beside his deathbed: "When you play music together, think of me, and I shall hear you."

Alfonso XIII (1886–1941), king of Spain, said when he was administered oxygen: "There are so many of the poor who have more need of it than I!"

Saint Benedict (c. 480–c. 550), abbot and founder of the Benedictine order, said to his sorrowing monks: "Don't grieve; I won't leave you alone."

George Lewis (1900–1968), the American jazz clarinetist of New Orleans, said to a friend who placed a crucifix in his hands as he was dying: "Departings are too hard. I'll be back after you!"

Vincent Lombardi (1913–1970) coached the Green Bay Packers and later the Washington Redskins. As he died of cancer, he whispered his very last words to his wife: "Happy anniversary! I love you."

Maurice Maeterlinck (1862–1949) was a Belgian dramatist, essayist and poet. On his deathbed he said to his wife: "For me this is quite natural. It is for you that I am concerned."

Henry Edward Manning (1808–1892), an English convert, became cardinal archbishop of Westminster and founded the Oblates of Saint Charles. He gave a friend a book that had belonged to his wife, who had died before he became a Catholic priest. "I know not to whom to leave this," he said. "I leave it to you. Into this little book my dearest wife wrote her prayers and meditations. Not a day has passed since her death on which I have not prayed and meditated from this book. All the good I may have done, all the good I may have been, I owe to her. Take precious care of it."

Saint Marcian (d. 304), a Roman soldier executed for being a Christian, told a friend: "Keep [my wife] away until it is all over. She must not see me die."

When his son came to him, just before he was beheaded, he gave him his blessing and said: "Lord Almighty, take this child into your special care."

Walker Percy, when his nurse asked whether she should wake his wife, replied: "No. She understands."

Pope Saint Pius X grieved deeply over the outbreak of World War I. Refusing to bless the armies of Austria-Hungary, he suffered a fatal heart attack after he dismissed Emperor Franz Josef from his presence, to whom he had said: "Get out of my sight! Get out of my sight! Away! Away! I grant blessing to no one who provokes the world to war!"

Just before the last rites, he offered up his life to God as a sacrifice, whispering: "I am dying for all the soldiers on the battlefield."

Saint Rita of Cascia (1381–1457), an Italian widow and mystic who became an Augustinian nun, is known as the patron saint of the impossible. She died looking at the crucifix, after having urged the nuns gathered around her: "May God bless you, and may you always remain in holy peace and love with your beloved spouse, Jesus Christ."

John Wayne (1907–1979), the popular American actor, was asked by his companion whether he knew her. He answered: "Of course I know who you are. You're my girl. I love you."

Saint Thomas Aquinas comforted a friend: "Don't be sad. We shall meet again in paradise."

Saint Hyacinth (1185–1257), a Polish Dominican missionary to Northern Europe, said to his compatriot, the prior: "Have faith in what I tell you. And try to believe that I shall never really leave Poland. I shall be with my beloved country until the end."

The prior asked, "Is our country to have many troubles in the future, Father?"

He replied: "Yes. But all will turn out well, Father Prior. Have no fear of that."

Saint John of God (1495–1550), the Italian lay founder of the Order of Brothers Hospitalers, dedicated his life to serving the sick and the poor. After receiving the last rites, he said:

> There are three things that make me uneasy. The first is that I have received so many graces from God, and have not recognized them, and have repaid them with so little of my own. The second is that after I am dead, I fear lest the poor women I have rescued, and the poor sinners I have reclaimed, may be treated badly. The third is that those who have trusted me with money, and whom I have not fully repaid, may suffer loss on my account.

Servant of God Titus Brandsma (1881–1942), a Dutch Carmelite priest, journalist and professor of philosophy, was appointed National Spiritual Advisor to the Dutch Catholic journalists. When he published a mandate declaring that a Catholic publication could not print Nazi propaganda and still claim to be Catholic, he was arrested by the Nazi occupiers and sent to the Dachau death camp.

He gave a rosary to the nurse who administered the injection that would kill him; it was his last possession. The nurse had been raised Catholic but had forgotten the prayers. He replied: "Well, if you can't say the first part, surely you can still say, 'Pray for us sinners.'"

Rogelio Gonzalez-Corzo (1932–1961) was a Catholic lay leader, agronomist engineer and activist in the Cuban resistance to Fidel Castro's Communist, anti-Catholic regime. In a letter to his family written minutes before he was executed, he said:

> Remember, I will be waiting for you in heaven. Be strong as I am strong even at this moment. And never forget that I am leaving this world worrying only about one thing: your spiritual life. Please do not neglect it for any reason.
>
> Under no circumstances should my fate be a motive for the weakening of your faith in God. Quite to the contrary, it should strengthen it. I have nothing more to say.

Sir Arthur Conan Doyle (1858–1930), the British author best known for his Sherlock Holmes mysteries, said to his nurse: "There ought to be a medal struck for you, inscribed, 'To the best of all nurses.'"

Robert Hugh Benson (1871–1914), English Catholic convert, priest and author, was concerned that his brother Arthur, standing nearby, would be disturbed by the sight of his death. The monsignor exclaimed: "Arthur! Don't look at me. Nurse, stand between my brother and me!"

Charlotte Corday (1768–1793) was a French patriot condemned to death in the French Revolution for assassinating Jean-Paul Marat, a bloodthirsty revolutionary leader. Before mounting the scaffold, she cut off a lock of her hair for the artist who had painted her portrait, saying: "Monsieur, I don't know how to thank you for your kindness. I have only this to offer you. Keep it as a remembrance of me."

Aloysius Schmitt (1909–1941), an American priest and Navy lieutenant from Iowa, was the first chaplain to die in World War II. When Pearl Harbor was bombed, he helped twelve shipmates on the USS *Oklahoma* escape through a porthole rather than escaping himself. His last words to them: "Go ahead, boys. I'm all right."

FOURTEEN

"Woman, Here Is Your Son"

The Communion of Saints

*When Jesus saw his
mother and the disciple
whom he loved standing
beside her, he said to his
mother, "Woman, here is
your son."*
—John 19:26

THE CHURCH HAS LONG RECOGNIZED THAT WHEN JESUS
gave Mary to John as his mother, he was giving her to us
all. Just as he said to her from the cross, "Woman, here is
your son," he says to her now from his throne in heaven,
"Woman, here are your children." Through this declaration our Lord established the foundation for a new family—the living, glorious reality we call the communion of
saints.

The night before his death, as he was praying for his
followers, he said to his Father: "I ask not only on behalf
of these, but also on behalf of those who will believe in me
through their word, that they may all be one" (John
17:20–21). In his dying words to his mother, the fulfillment of that prayer had its beginning. The oneness of
those who are in Christ—those of every generation until
the end of time—springs from a family's love, flowing in

superabundance between the Father, the Son and the Spirit, spilling over into a mother's immaculate heart and out to her thirsty children (v. 26).

Death has no power to divide the members of this extraordinary household. It's only a stairway from one floor of the family mansion up to the next (see John 14:2–3). Whether the redeemed live on earth, in heaven or in preparation for heaven, their unity allows them access to one another for a sharing of spiritual goods. And because this unity is a communion of divine love, their prayers and good works are energized by God's own power to heal and purify, strengthen and bless.

A firm confidence in these realities is evident in many Catholics' last words. Some call upon the mother Jesus has given them, speaking to her in their last moments just as he did, claiming the privileges of a son or daughter in need. Many of them have said the rosary all their lives, asking her to pray for them "in the hour of [their] death." Now that the hour has come, they trust that she will be close by to help them. At the end of his life, Padre Pio invoked Jesus and his mother, as did the missionary explorer Father Jacques Marquette.

A number of Catholics have spent their last breath calling the names of the Holy Family, the circle of love at the heart of the communion of saints: Jesus, Mary and Joseph, the patron saint of a happy death. Among these were the American Saint Elizabeth Ann Seton and the Polish military general Casimir Pulaski, who helped colonists win their freedom in the American Revolution.

The dying may also call on the aid of a saint who has been a personal favorite throughout life or the patron of a particular order or nation: Saint Benedict, Saint Joan of Arc, Saint Anne, Saint Claude. The Italian composer Gaetano Donizetti, apparently convinced of his deceased wife's sainthood, asked for her help: "I shall be miserable until she intercedes with God for my death and our eternal reunion."

Some last words are requests that prayers and Masses be said for the departing. They recognize, as King Henry VII of England put it, how "behoofful it is to be prayed for" on our way to heaven.

Finally, those with good reason to be more confident that their passage into heaven will be swift offer their assurances to those left behind. Once they are standing face-to-face with God, these dying men and women insist, they will entrust to him the needs of loved ones still on earth. Such is the meaning, for example, of Saint Thérèse's famous promise to send down "a shower of roses."

The church has documented numerous miracles obtained through the invocation of these and other saints throughout the ages. They leave no doubt that the members of the family in heaven are busy keeping their commitments to those of us who have yet to take the stairway up to meet them.

* * *

Saint Alphonsus Liguori (1696–1787) was the Italian bishop and theologian who founded the Redemptorist Congregation. As he lay dying he asked a companion, "Give me the picture of our Lady." Then, gazing at it, he prayed the Hail Mary. Its concluding petition was his last prayer: "Holy Mary, Mother of God, pray for us sinners, now and at the hour of our death."

Venerable Maria Teresa of Jesus Quevado (1930–1950) was a Spanish Carmelite of Charity who consecrated herself to Mary at age thirteen and joined the order at age eighteen, shortly before she died of tubercular meningitis. Her last words were spoken with a bright smile: "How beautiful, O Mary, how beautiful you are!"

Ernesto Ruffini (1888–1967), cardinal archbishop of Palermo, Sicily, whispered this last act of faith: "I am dying, but I am tranquil. I am with the Madonna."

Saint Bernadette Soubirous (1844–1879) was the French Sister of Charity whose Marian visions (when she was only fourteen) have brought millions of pilgrims for healing and other favors to Lourdes, France. On the day she died of tuberculosis, the Mother Superior said, "I will ask our Immaculate Mother to give you some consolation."

Bernadette replied: "No. No consolation, but strength and patience. All this can be used for heaven. I saw her! I saw her! Oh, how beautiful she was, and how I long to see her again!" Her last words were "Mother of God, pray for me, poor sinner! Mother of God, pray for me, poor sinner!"

Blessed Pauline-Marie Jaricot (1799–1862) was the French founder of the Society of the Propagation of the Faith and the Association of the Living Rosary. Stretching her arms out to a statue of our Lady, she said: "Mary, my mother, I am all yours."

William the Conqueror (c. 1027–1088) died with this invocation: "I commend myself to our blessed Lady, Mary the Mother of God, that she by her holy intercession may reconcile me to her Son, our Lord Jesus Christ."

Jules Mazarin (1602–1661), a French cardinal and prime minister, prayed: "Ah, Blessed Virgin! Have pity on me and receive my soul."

Saint Francis Xavier called to Jesus for mercy, then whispered: "O Virgin Mother of God, remember me."

Saint Gemma Galgani, a humble Italian servant girl, mystic and stigmatist who died of tuberculosis, addressed our Lord and our Lady: "O Jesus, you see that I am at the end of my strength. I can bear no more. If it be your holy will, take me. Mother, I commend my soul into your hands. Do ask Jesus to be merciful to me."

Pope John Paul II made as his final declaration—according to his personal secretary, who was present when he died—the words of his papal motto, an act of personal consecration to our Lady: *"Totus tuus,"* "Totally yours."

Blessed Miguel Pro told a friend not long before his arrest and execution: "If I am ever caught, be prepared to ask me for things when I am in heaven!"

Ten days before his death by a firing squad, he composed a prayer to our Lady that ends with these words: "For my life, I covet the jeers and mockery of Calvary; the slow agony of your Son, the contempt, the ignominy, the infamy of His Cross. I wish to stand at your side, most sorrowful Virgin, strengthening my spirit with your tears, consummating my sacrifice with your martyrdom, sustaining my heart with your solitude, loving my God and your God with the immolation of my being."

Robert Hugh Benson and **Saint John Bosco** both expired with the words "Jesus, Mary and Joseph, I give you my heart and soul!"

Pierre de Bérulle (1575–1629) was a French cardinal, theologian, mystic and writer who established seventeen seminaries and reportedly worked miraculous cures. At the end he prayed: "May Jesus and Mary bless, rule and govern."

Charles VIII (1470–1498), king of France, died of accidental head injuries. He cried: "My God, the Virgin Mary, my lord Saint Claude and my lord Saint Blaise, they help me!"

Blessed Louis Martin (1823–1894), layman and father of Saint Thérèse of Lisieux, said to his children: "O children, do pray for me. Beg Saint Joseph that I might die a saintly death."

Marie-Clément Staub (1876–1936) was a French Assumptionist missionary priest to America who founded the Sisters of Saint Joan of Arc. The morning of the day he died, he said to the novices of the order: "Only the valiant become saints! So you must become holy and valiant souls! I desire so much that you become like Saint Joan....I shall speak to her for you."

Philip I (1052–1108), king of France, reportedly died of obesity. His last wishes:

> I know the kings of France are buried in the Church of Saint Denis, but I have been too great a sinner for my body to lie alongside so great a martyr. I fear indeed that my sins have been so great that I shall be delivered up to the devil....
>
> I have always revered Saint Benedict. Dying, I call upon this father of these monks and ask to be buried in his church by the [River] Loire. He is filled with mercy and goodness. He welcomes sinners who desire to repent and be reconciled to God within his rule.

Mary Pickford (1892–1979), a Canadian-born film star and producer, was known as "America's Sweetheart." Just before she died she pointed to pictures of her parents and of Christ and whispered: "There's Mama and Papa. And there's Jesus."

Richard I died of an infected wound suffered in combat. He asked that his mother, Queen Eleanor of Aquitaine, have Masses said for him: "I place all my trust, after God, in you, that you will make provision for my soul's welfare with motherly care, to the utmost of your power."

Theobald Mathew (1790–1856) was an Irish Capuchin priest and temperance advocate who inspired thousands to "take the pledge" to abstain from alcohol. On his deathbed he begged his brother: "Promise me, oh, promise me that you will remember me in your prayers during the Holy Sacrifice."

Saint Monica said to Saint Augustine as she lay dying: "This only I ask of you: that you should remember me at the altar of the Lord wherever you may be."

Isabella I (1451–1504), queen of Spain, said to those in tears around her deathbed: "Do not weep for me, nor waste your time in fruitless prayers for my recovery, but pray rather for the salvation of my soul."

Charles X (1757–1836), king of France, said to his grandchildren: "May God protect you, my children. Walk in the paths of justice. Do not forget me. Pray for me sometimes."

Pope Leo X (1475–1521) was a patron of the arts and the nemesis of the Protestant Reformer Martin Luther. Dying from a sudden illness, he asked those around him: "Pray for me. I want to make you all happy."

Blessed Damien de Veuster was asked as he lay dying of leprosy contracted through his work: "When you are there, Father, you won't forget those whom you are leaving orphans?"

"Oh, no," he replied. "If I have any credit with God, I shall intercede for all who are in the leprosarium."

Gloria María Elizondo García (d. 1966) was a Mexican lay apostle to the poor who later entered the Congregation of the Catechist Missionary Mothers of the Poor and was elected superior general. Dying from cancer, she received last rites with her sisters gathered around her, to whom she said:

"Do not think that I am going to forget you. If here on earth every day I look out for each one of you and for your families, there above [in heaven] where I will have no other occupation, how much more will I desire what is good for you! I promise you that I will intercede for you. There I will be able to do for the congregation much more than I can do here."

Blessed Junípero Serra declared: "I promise, if the Lord in his infinite mercy grants me eternal happiness, which I do not deserve because of my sins and faults, that I shall pray for all and for the conversions of so many whom I leave unconverted."

Saint Ignatius Loyola (1491–1556) was a Basque soldier who became a priest, spiritual writer and one of the founders of the Society of Jesus (the Jesuits). He sent his secretary to the pope with these instructions: "Tell him that my hour has come, and that I ask his benediction. Tell him that if I go to a place where my prayers are of any avail, as I trust, I shall not fail to pray for him, as I have indeed unfailingly, even when I had most occasion to pray for myself."

Saint Dominic de Guzmán said to his brothers: "Don't let my departure in the flesh trouble you, my sons, and don't doubt that I shall serve you better dead than alive!"

Saint Columba (c. 521–597), Irish missionary to the Picts of Scotland, said to the brothers of his monastery on the island of Iona: "Have unfeigned charity among yourselves, and if you thus follow the example of the Holy Fathers, God the comforter of the good will be your Helper. And I, abiding with him, will intercede for you, and he will not only give you sufficient to supply the wants of this present life but will also bestow on you the good and eternal rewards which are laid up for those that keep his commandments."

FIFTEEN

"I Am Coming to You"
VISIONS AND VOICES, OMENS AND PREMONITIONS

> *I will not leave you*
> *orphaned; I am coming to*
> *you. In a little while the*
> *world will no longer see*
> *me, but you will see me.*
> —John 14:18–19

IN HIS FINAL ENCOURAGEMENTS TO HIS FRIENDS, JESUS promised that after his death, he would not leave them "orphaned"; he would come back, and they would see him. He kept that promise in a number of ways: through his appearances after the Resurrection (see 1 Corinthians 15:4–8); through the descent of his indwelling Spirit (Galatians 4:6); through fellowship with other believers wherever they may gather (Matthew 18:20). Above all, Jesus comes to us through the graces of the sacraments, whose summit is his real presence in the Eucharist (Luke 22:19–20).

At the same time our Lord spoke of still another coming to his people: his second advent at the end of the world. "They will see 'the Son of Man coming on the clouds of heaven' with power and great glory" (Matthew 24:30). This event may seem to lie in the distant future, and perhaps it does. Nevertheless, as Saint John Chrysostom reminds us, "even if the day when the whole world ends never overtakes us, the end of each of us is right at the door." In a sense Christ's advent takes place personally for each of us when we die.

"I go to prepare a place for you," Jesus told his disciples the night before he died. "And if I go and prepare a place for you, I will come again and will take you to myself, so that where I am, there you may be also" (see John 14:2–3).

Those words received their initial fulfillment at the death of Saint Stephen. Having been stoned by a mob, he was about to expire when "he gazed into heaven and saw the glory of God and Jesus standing at the right hand of God. 'Look,' he said, 'I see the heavens opened and the Son of Man standing at the right hand of God!'" (Acts 7:55–56).

For Saint Stephen the end of the world had come. The Son of Man was coming back for him in glory, and the martyr saw him coming, as his Lord had promised. With his place now prepared, he yielded his spirit to Jesus, forgave his murderers and breathed his last (vv. 59–60). The first Christian martyr thus became the first Christian to experience a vision in the hour of death.

But Stephen was by no means the last. Numerous accounts of last words show that the dying sometimes behold their Lord at their side or hear his voice. Others tell of seeing or hearing angels or saints. That should come as no surprise, as Jesus said these holy ones would accompany him when he returns to judge the world (see Matthew 24:30–31). Might they not be with him as well when he comes to take one of us home?

Jesus made yet another promise the night before his

crucifixion, this one specifically to Saint Peter. It was a consolation but also a warning, chilling in its implications: "Satan has demanded to sift all of you like wheat, but I have prayed for you that your own faith may not fail" (Luke 22:31–32).

Whether the devil actually appeared to the apostle at some point, we don't know. But the last words of many Christians suggest that the enemy of our souls does indeed have a habit of showing up to test the faith of the dying, through apparitions, voices or some other means. Some respond calmly, maintaining a trust in the One who has protected them for a lifetime. Others are terrified, but the vision seems to drive them to a deeper dependence on God's grace, a firmer confidence in Christ's victory. All of them, we may hope, find in the end that their Lord indeed prayed for them, and their faith did not fail.

Finally, we should note that those near death sometimes have a premonition—or interpret some event as an omen—of what is to come. Whether or not these experiences have a supernatural origin is of course difficult to judge. Whatever their source, our Lord can certainly use such experiences to ready people for his arrival. And those who know death is at hand can make the most of that knowledge to prepare themselves accordingly.

* * *

Saint Ambrose (c. 340–397), the celebrated preacher, bishop of Milan and doctor of the church, reported as he was dying: "I see the Lord Jesus at my bedside, smiling at me."

Saint Anthony of Padua sang a hymn as he was dying, and afterward he kept his eyes firmly fixed toward heaven. At last the friar who was supporting him asked him what it was he was looking at so intently. He replied simply: "I see my Lord."

Saint Clare of Assisi (1193–1253) founded the Poor Clares in association with Saint Francis. She said to one of her spiritual daughters just before she breathed her last: "O daughter, can you see the King of Glory that I see?" One of the other sisters then had a vision of a retinue of virgins dressed in white, wearing golden crowns and coming to escort Clare to her Bridegroom.

Blessed Francisco Marto (1908–1919), one of the three child visionaries of Fátima, Portugal, died in the Spanish flu epidemic, in accordance with a prophecy the children had received from our Lady. Just before he died he told his mother: "Look, Mama! What a pretty light there, near the door! Now I don't see it anymore. Mama, bless me and forgive me for all the trouble I have caused you in my life."

Blessed Jacinta Marto (1910–1920), sister of Francisco and also one of the visionaries of Fátima, died in the same epidemic, as foretold by our Lady. She told her nurse: "I have seen our Lady. She told me that she was going to come for me very soon and take away my pains. I am going to die. I want the Sacrament."

The nurse hurried to get the priest, but when she came back, Jacinta was dead.

Saint Elizabeth (1271–1336), queen consort of Denis, king of Portugal, founded hospitals, orphanages and homes for abandoned women. As she was dying she had a vision of the Blessed Mother. She said to her attendants: "Draw up a chair for the radiant Lady in white who is coming! O Mary, Mother of Grace!"

Venerable Galileo Nicolini (1882–1897) was an Italian boy who entered the Passionist novitiate at age fourteen and died of tuberculosis soon afterward. On the morning of the day he died, he asked the infirmarian to light all the candles around an image of our Lady and to call the religious brothers to gather. He prayed the Hail Mary several times, then pointed at the image of our Lady and exclaimed, "The saints!" He motioned for the brothers to make way, sat up as if to greet visitors, then closed his eyes and sank back into his pillow, dead.

Saint Martin de Porres (1579–1639) was a Peruvian Dominican lay brother known for his mystical gifts. After the administration of the last rites, he was urged in his agony to invoke Saint Dominic. He replied: "It would be useless to ask him to come. He is already here with Saint Vincent Ferrer."

Saint Thomas Aquinas reported a few months before he died a mystical vision of angels. Though he had written many volumes in his lifetime, he never wrote again. He concluded: "All I have written seems like so much straw, compared to that which I have seen and what has been revealed to me."

Saint Teresa of Jesus (Avila) said at the end: "Over my spirit flash and float in divine radiance the bright and glorious visions of the world to which I go."

Saint Goar (c. 519–575), the patron saint of the River Rhine, was a priest and religious hermit of Aquitaine known far and wide for his great holiness. Before he died he had a vision of things to come in the area around his hermitage in Oberwesel, Germany: "Here shall my Savior be known in all the simplicity of his doctrines. Ah, would that I might witness it, but I have seen these things in a vision. But I faint! I am weary! My earthly journey is finished. Receive my blessing. Go and be kind to one another."

William Allingham (1824–1889), an Irish poet, said as he was dying: "I am seeing things that you know nothing of!"

Jean-Jacques Rousseau (1712–1778), the French philosopher and political theorist, paced the floor in exquisite pain from illness. He suddenly exclaimed: "Being of Beings, God! See how pure the sky is! There is not a single cloud! Do you see that its gates are open and that God awaits me?" Then he fell to the floor and died.

Saint Dominic Savio (1842–1857), an Italian student and assistant of Saint John Bosco, founder of the Salesian order, was comforting his parents as he died of pneumonia. He said: "Surely you're not crying, Mom, at seeing me go to heaven! Look, Dad, look! Can't you see the wonderful…beautiful…."

Louis XVII, the French dauphin who died at the age of ten, said to an attendant just before he expired: "The music is so beautiful. Listen. In the midst of all those voices, I recognize my mother's."

Edmund Husserl told his nurse minutes before his death: "Oh, I have seen something so wonderful! Quick, write it down!"

She ran to get writing materials, but by the time she came back, he was dead.

Luigi Pirandello (1867–1936), the Italian novelist and dramatist, suffered a night of delirious hallucinations. He told his son a few hours before he died: "I look forward to writing down, in a few days, all that I imagined in those few hours."

James Gibbons (1834–1921), cardinal archbishop of Baltimore, said to some of his aides: "You do not know how I suffer. The imagination is a powerful thing. My reason tells me that the images which rise before me have no foundation in fact. Faith must ever be the consolation of all men. Without faith we can accomplish little. Faith bears us up in our trials."

Saint Martin of Tours, harassed by an apparition of Satan, cried out just before he died: "What are you doing here, bloodthirsty beast? You will find nothing in me that is yours, accursed angel. It is Abraham's bosom that is to receive me!"

Henry V (1387–1422), king of England, died of dysentery at age thirty-four. He shouted to the devil: "You lie! You lie! My portion is with the Lord Jesus!" Then, clutching a crucifix, he prayed: "Into your hands, O Lord. You have redeemed my end."

Saint Catherine of Genoa (1447–1510), the Italian mystic known for her *Treatise on Purgatory*, saw an apparition of Satan. She cried out, "Drive away the beast that is looking for food!"

Saint Louis de Montfort (1673–1716), the French Jesuit priest and founder of the Missionaries of the Company of Mary, was known for his powerful preaching. Apparently responding to an apparition of Satan by his deathbed, he exclaimed: "No, no! It is useless for you to attack me. Jesus and Mary are with me. I have come to the end of my life. It is over now, and I shall never sin again."

Pope Alexander VI (1431–1503), a Spaniard notorious for his immoral behavior, saw Satan in the form of an ape running around his sickroom. When a cardinal offered to catch the animal, he warned: "Let it alone, for it is the devil!" Then he said to the devil: "I am coming, I am coming. It is just. But wait a little."

Jean-François Millet (1814–1875), a pre-Impressionist French painter known for his scenes of ordinary life, was watching a deer, wounded by hunters, fall outside his window. He observed: "It is an omen. The poor beast which comes to die beside me warns me that I too am about to die."

Henry IV (1367–1413), king of England, had traveled to places far and wide, including the Holy Land. When he was told that the chamber in which he lay ill was called Jerusalem, he replied: "Praise be given to the Father of heaven, for now I know that I shall die here in this chamber, according to the prophecy declared of me, that I should depart this life in Jerusalem."

Michel de Nostredame (1503–1566), known better as Nostradamus, was a French physician and astrologer who made accurate predictions about the fortunes of famous contemporaries. His book of rhymed prophecies, though obscure in meaning and variously interpreted, still occupies many who seek to peer into the future. In response to a priest friend's farewell greeting, "Until tomorrow," Nostradamus answered: "You will not find me alive at sunrise." He died that night.

Saint Catherine Labouré (1806–1876) was a sister of Saint Vincent de Paul in Paris. Her visions led to the creation and promotion of the Miraculous Medal. When her niece was leaving, promising to return the next morning, Catherine said: "You shall see me, but I shall not see you, for I won't be here."

Oscar-Claude Monet (1840–1926), the French Impressionist painter, told a friend two weeks before he died that he had planted some seedlings in the garden, then added: "You will see all that in the spring, but I won't be here anymore."

Wolfgang Amadeus Mozart (1756–1791), the celebrated Austrian composer, was composing a *Requiem*. As he was dying he said to his friends: "Did I not tell you that I was writing this for myself?"

Saint Philip Neri (1515–1595) was an Italian priest, mystic, miracle worker and founder of the Oratorians. He was known as "the Apostle of Rome" for his preaching in that city, which brought about many conversions. Future events were sometimes revealed to him, as was the timing of his death. Preparing himself for bed the night he was to die from illness, he said: "Well, last of all, one has to die. Three and two are five, three and three are six, and then we shall go."

Blessed María Romero Menenses (1902–1977), a Nicaraguan Salesian nun known as "the Social Apostle of Costa Rica," devoted her life to caring for the poor. One day, on vacation at the beach, she looked out to sea and said: "I see God in every drop of water in this sea. How beautiful it would be to die facing the ocean!" A few hours later she did just that, dying from a heart attack.

Venerable Antonio Margil (1657–1726) was a Spanish Franciscan superior and missionary to Mexico famed for his preaching. As he lay dying after preaching a mission in Mexico City, an image of Our Lady of Remedies was placed before him. He looked at it and prayed: "Good-bye, Lady, till tomorrow." The next afternoon he died.

Saint Isaac Jogues (1607–1646) was a French Jesuit missionary to the Native Americans of Quebec, one of the Martyrs of North America. He was captured by a war party of Iroquois, who murdered two of his companions, and then he endured a year of torture and mutilation at their hands. He escaped and made it back to France but requested to be sent again to Quebec.

While ministering there, he was asked to accompany some Hurons on a peace mission to the village where he had been taken captive and tortured. Just before he left, he wrote his superiors in France: "My heart tells me that, if I am the one to be sent on this mission, I shall go, but I shall not return. But I would be happy if our Lord wished to complete the sacrifice where he began it." He was indeed murdered during that visit to the village where he had been tortured years before.

Saint John of the Cross (1542–1591) was the Spanish Carmelite mystic and spiritual writer known especially for his work *The Dark Night of the Soul*. The day before his death he predicted: "At midnight tonight I shall be saying Matins in heaven." When the bell was rung signaling Matins—the first office of prayer in the day—he shouted: "Glory be to God!" and took his last breath.

Servant of God Frank Parater (1897–1920) was a godly young American seminarian from Virginia who died of rheumatic fever while attending the North American College in Rome. A sealed envelope among his belongings, entitled "My Last Will," bore the instructions "To be opened only in the case of my death." He had written it only two months before, when he was enjoying good health with no sign of the approaching illness. The document said in part:

> I have nothing to leave or give but my life, and this I have consecrated to the Sacred Heart to be used as He wills. I have offered my all for the conversions to God of non-Catholics in Virginia. This is what I live for and, in case of death, what I die for.
>
> Death is not unpleasant to me, but the most beautiful and welcome event of my life. Death is the messenger of God come to tell us that our novitiate is ended and to welcome us to the real life.
>
> Melancholic or morbid sentimentality is not the cause of my writing this, for I love life here, the college, the men, and Rome itself. But I have desired to die and be buried with the saints. I dare not ask God to take me lest I should be ungrateful or be trying to shirk the higher responsibilities of life; but I shall never have less to answer for—perhaps never to be better ready to meet my Maker, my God, my All.

SIXTEEN

"I Am Deeply Grieved"
GRIEF AND REGRET

> *He... began to be grieved
> and agitated. Then he
> said to them, "I am deeply
> grieved, even to death."*
> —Matthew 26:37–38

WE WILL NEVER KNOW FULLY JUST HOW HEAVY WAS THE
burden Jesus carried in his soul as he knelt to pray in
Gethsemane. But we do know the weight was brutally
crushing, enough to press blood from the pores of his skin
(see Luke 22:44). On his shoulders he bore not only the
pain of the whole world but the sins of the whole world
as well (John 1:29). And he grieved as only the holy can
grieve for the sins of others; he felt the outrage of evil as
only the heart of God can feel it.

It was a grief, he told his friends, "even to death."
Perhaps the sorrow was in fact more deadly than the
whips and the nails: physicians studying the crucifixion
accounts note how the blood and water flowing from his
pierced side (see John 19:34) indicate that he may well
have died, quite literally, of a broken heart.

Sometimes the final words of Christians reflect a
share in Christ's dying sorrow, though most often they are

grieving not for the sins of others but their own. At the end of life comes the long-feared or long-ignored reckoning; their sins of commission and omission, their failures and errors catch up with them. Some feel shame and respond with a heartfelt confession. Others, apparently lacking a genuine sense of remorse, seem to find room only for regret.

"If only..." may be the saddest last words of all. But for those of us not yet at death's door, they provide an oft-needed reminder to reexamine our lives while we still have time to reform them.

* * *

Philip III (1578–1621), king of Spain, said as he died: "Oh, would to God I had never reigned! Oh, that those years in my kingdom I had lived instead a solitary life in the wilderness! Oh, that I had lived alone with God! How much more secure should I have died. With how much more confidence should I have gone to the throne of God! What does all my glory profit but that I have so much the more torment in my death?"

Maggie Teyte (1888–1976) was an English operatic soprano. Not long before she died, she said: "I have not lived like a Catholic, but I hope I shall die like one."

Jules Cardinal Mazarin died with these words: "Oh, were I permitted to live again, I would sooner be the humblest wretch in the ranks of mendicants than a courtier."

Lope de Vega (1562–1635) was a Spanish Franciscan priest and dramatic poet. He observed: "True glory is in virtue. Ah! I would willingly give all the applause I have received to have performed one good action more."

Thomas Wolsey (1475–1530), an English cardinal and statesman, died just before his trial for treason, a charge resulting from his opposition to the plans of King Henry VIII to divorce Catherine of Aragon. He declared: "If I had served God as diligently as I have done the king, he would not have given me over in my gray hairs. But this is the just reward that I must receive for my diligent pains and studies that I have had to do him service, and not regarding my services to God."

Cesare Borgia (c. 1475–1507) was the Italian cardinal archbishop of Valencia and a statesman. He concluded: "I have taken care of everything in the course of my life, only not for death—and now I have to die completely unprepared."

Stephen Gardiner (c. 1482–1555), bishop of Winchester and Lord Chancellor of England, was something of a political opportunist. When Henry VIII broke the Church of England away from Rome, Gardiner went along with the schism and signed the renunciation of obedience to Rome. But when the Catholic Queen Mary came to power, he supported her in the killing of Protestants. Dying of a painful disease, he confessed: "I have denied with Peter; I have gone out with Peter; but not yet have I wept with Peter."

Henry IV (1050–1106), king of Germany and Holy Roman Emperor, remarked: "O how unhappy I am who squandered such great treasures in vain! How happy I could have been if I had given these things to the poor!"

Sophie Arnould (1744–1802) was a French opera singer. When her priest commented on "the bad times" she had been through, she replied: "Oh, the times were good. It was I who was so unhappy."

Vincent Foster (d. 1993) was a United States attorney and associate of President Bill Clinton. His alleged suicide prompted rumors that he had been assassinated as part of a political cover-up. He left a note that said: "Here [in Washington], ruining people is considered sport."

Artur Seyss-Inquart (1892–1946) was an Austrian-born Nazi war criminal condemned to death by hanging at the Nuremburg trials. He gave as his last statement: "I hope that this execution is the last act of the tragedy of the Second World War and that the lesson taken from this world war will be that peace and understanding should exist between peoples. I believe in Germany."

Maria Eva Duarte Perón (1919–1952), the Argentine political leader, died from cancer. She said to her maid a few hours before she fell into a coma: "I have never felt happy in this life."

Pope Julius II (1443–1513) was known as the "Terrible Pope" because of the many wars he waged as leader of the papal states. He lamented: "Would to God that I had never been pope, or at least that I could have turned all the arms of religion against the enemies of the Holy See!"

Evariste Galois (1811–1832) was a French mathematician. Wounded in a duel, he said to his friends: "Don't cry. I need all my courage to die at twenty."

Henry VII, king of England, lay dying of tuberculosis. He said to his attendants: "If it should please God to send me life, you should find me a new, changed man."

Leonardo da Vinci (1450–1519), the celebrated Italian genius of art and science, died without having found the perfection he so desired. He lamented: "I have offended God and mankind in not having worked at my art as I ought to have done."

James Joyce had renounced the Christian faith. His last words were a poignant question: "Does nobody understand?"

Henry VIII (1491–1547), king of England, was responsible for the martyrdom of his friend Saint Thomas More and others who refused to apostasize, as well as the plunder of Catholic monasteries and churches. His last words: "All is lost. Monks, monks, monks! So, now all is gone—empire, body, soul!"

Henry Beaufort (c. 1374–1447), an English cardinal and statesman, lamented: "Will not all my riches save me? What! Is there no bribing death?"

Marie Thérèse of Austria (1638–1683) was a Spanish princess who married King Louis XIV, France's "Sun King." As she died from efforts to treat an abscess, she lamented: "Since I became queen, I have not known a single happy day."

Peter Abelard (1079–1142) was a French philosopher and theologian. His last words: "I do not know."

Claude-Frédéric Bastiat died saying: "I am not able to explain myself."

Catherine de' Medici (1519–1589), queen consort of King Henry II of France, was the mother of three kings who succeeded each other without heirs, bringing to an end the House of Valois. Her last words: "I am crushed in the ruins of the House!"

Ludwig van Beethoven, in one account of his death, said bitterly, "Friends, applaud! The comedy is over."

Ernesto "Che" Guevara (1928–1967), the Argentine revolutionary, was captured and shot by the Bolivian army while leading a guerilla movement in South America. Confessing his shame over having been captured alive, he said: "Do not worry, Captain. It is all over. I have failed."

Henry II (1133–1189), king of England, was indirectly responsible for the death of Saint Thomas Becket. He suppressed a rebellion by some of his sons but died while preparing to suppress another by his favorite son, John. Learning of John's role in the conspiracy against him, he said: "Let the rest go as it will. Now I care not what becomes of me. Shame, shame on a conquered king!"

Joseph II (1741–1790), Austrian Holy Roman Emperor, was in frequent conflict with the church because of his efforts to control nearly every aspect of its life. Inevitably his "reforms" failed. Before he died he gave instructions that his epitaph should be: "Here lies Joseph, who was unsuccessful in all his undertakings."

Maurice, Comte de Saxe (1696–1750), was the marshal of France. He said to his physician: "Doctor, life is but a dream. Mine has been beautiful, but it has been brief."

François Rabelais reportedly said: "Draw the curtain; the farce is ended."

Francis Thompson (1859–1907) was the British poet best known for "The Hound of Heaven." As he died he repeated a line from one of his poems: "My withered dreams ... my withered dreams."

Oscar Wilde became Catholic toward the end of his life. His grave bears the inscription:

And alien tears will fill for him
Pity's long broken urn
For his mourners will be outcast men
And outcasts always mourn.

SEVENTEEN

"You Were Not Willing!"
Pride and Impenitence

> *Jerusalem, Jerusalem, the city that kills the prophets and stones those who are sent to it! How often have I desired to gather your children together as a hen gathers her brood under her wings, and you were not willing!*
> —Matthew 23:37

A MEDIEVAL FRENCH NOBLEMAN OF THE HOUSE OF Du Châtelet left express directions about where his body was to be laid to rest. Members of his family were customarily buried under the floor of the church at Neufchâteau. But he insisted that he must be entombed instead in one of the church's columns.

His reason for such unusual instructions? "So that the vulgar," he said, "may not walk about upon me."

"You are dust," the Lord says, "and to dust you shall return" (Genesis 3:19). Such snobbery this is from a pile of dust!

In the hour of death all grounds for arrogance or vanity are swiftly passing away, yet some still refuse to humble themselves. Their Lord calls them, as he once called the people of Jerusalem, to lay aside their pride and run to him for refuge, as helpless chicks run to a mother hen. But now as then, many are unwilling to do so (see Matthew 23:37).

For some the last words display a brazen haughtiness: Pope Clement XII said to the priest who offered to hear his confession: "I have no fault of any kind." King Louis XIV of France demanded: "Has God forgotten everything I've done for him?"

For others the pride seems less scandalous because of its shallowness, a vanity that is nevertheless ugly because it is so petty. Thus Jean-Phillipe Rameau, a French composer, said to the attending priest: "Why the devil do you have to sing to me, priest? Your voice is out of tune!" Duchess Pauline Bonaparte, the sister of Napoleon I, looked in a mirror and said: "She may be dying, but she was always beautiful!"

Most chilling are the final pronouncements of those whose pride has hardened into impenitence. They blaspheme; they defy God and his law; they justify themselves. They set themselves in their Maker's place, daring to judge his ways, mock his name, deny his existence. We must leave their souls in heaven's merciful hands. Perhaps between the last word and the last heartbeat there was a moment of grace, a flash of interior repentance. God alone knows.

In the meantime, in their deaths we glimpse the pitfalls of pride, that most deadly of the seven deadly sins. Such scenes should remind us that in the light of eternity, we are dust: beloved by God, to be sure, but dust nonetheless. And it is not at all fitting for dust to be proud.

* * *

Auguste Comte (1798–1857), the French philosopher known as the founder of modern sociology, said of his approaching demise: "What an irreparable loss!"

Godwin (d. 1053), earl of Wessex, was accused by King Edward the Confessor of murdering his brother. He replied: "I am as safe in swallowing this morsel of bread, as I am guiltless of the deed." He choked on the bread and died.

Louis XV, king of France, led a life of personal debauchery. He declared proudly: "I have caused more than a hundred thousand Masses to be said for the repose of unhappy souls, so that I flatter myself I have not been a very bad Christian."

Thomas de Mahay (1744–1790), Marquis de Favras, was one of the many victims of the French Revolution. Reading over his death sentence, written out by a clerk of the court, he said: "I see that you have made three spelling mistakes."

François de Malherbe (1555–1628), a French poet and critic, interrupted the priest at his bedside who was trying to describe heaven: "Do not speak of it any more. Your bad style leaves me disgusted."

Antoine Watteau (1684–1721) was a French painter. When the priest came to administer the last rites, the artist complained: "Take this crucifix away from me! How could an artist portray so poorly the features of a God?"

Jeanne Antoinette Poisson (1721–1764), Marquise de Pompadour, was the mistress of Louis XV. Dying of pneumonia, with her last breath she called out: "Wait a second!" Then, dabbing rouge on her pale cheeks, she died.

Joachim Murat (1767–1815) was a French cavalry commander who became the king of Naples. Just before his execution for supporting Napoleon, he said: "Soldiers, do your duty. Aim for the heart, but spare the face."

Georges-Jacques Danton (1759–1794) was a French revolutionary arrested by his fellow revolutionary and former friend Robespierre on charges of disloyalty. Just before he was beheaded, he said to his executioners: "Above all, don't forget to show my head to the people. It's well worth having a look at!"

Rodrigo Calderón (c. 1576–1621), a Spanish courtier, was imprisoned and tortured by his political enemies. His arrogance as he finally faced the hangman gave rise to the Spanish proverb "to be haughtier than Don Rodrigo on the scaffold." His last words: "All my life I have carried myself gracefully."

Claude Henri de Saint-Simon (1760–1825) was the founder of French socialism. He sought to remove dogma from the Christian faith and reduce it to a social program, but his predictions about the future of his movement were overconfident: "All my life is comprised in this one thought: to guarantee to all men the freest development of their faculties. The future is ours!"

Joseph-Ernest Renan (1823–1892), a French historian, philosopher and Orientalist, was similarly overconfident of his school of thought. Having come to deny the supernatural realm and to doubt that Christ was God, he proclaimed the day before he died: "I die in the communion of mankind and the church of the future!"

William Tecumseh Sherman (1820–1891) was a Union general in the Civil War known for his harsh "scorched earth" tactics against the civilian population of Georgia, where he remains a despised figure for his cruelty. When asked what inscription he wanted on his gravestone, he said: "Faithful and honorable, faithful and honorable."

Voltaire, the French author and skeptic, reacted vehemently when a priest came into his sickroom, asking whether he would at last confess the divinity of Jesus Christ. He reportedly blurted out in anger: "Jesus Christ! Jesus Christ! Never speak to me again about that man! Let me die in peace!"

Joan Crawford (1908–1977), the American actress, left the church many years before she died. As she was on her deathbed, she said to her housekeeper, who had begun to pray aloud: "Damn it! How dare you ask God to help me!"

Pietro Perugino (1446–1523), an Italian Renaissance painter, gave his reason for refusing to see a priest as he lay dying: "I am curious to see what happens in the next world to one who dies without having made a confession."

Ramón María Narváez (1800–1868) was a Spanish general and prime minister. When the attending priest confessor exhorted him to forgive his enemies, he retorted: "I do not have to forgive my enemies. I have had them all shot."

Niccolò Machiavelli (1469–1527) was a Florentine Renaissance diplomat and political philosopher whose name has become synonymous with state policies—especially craft and deceit—carried out purely for the sake of expediency, with no regard for morality. Characteristically he said: "I desire to go to hell and not to heaven. In the former I shall enjoy the company of popes, kings and princes, while in the latter are only beggars, monks and apostles."

Adrienne LeCouvreur (1692–1730) was a French actress and the mistress of Maurice, Comte de Saxe; she was reputedly poisoned by a rival. When asked by the priest to repent, she pointed to the bust of the Comte de Saxe and declared defiantly: "There is my universe, my hope, my deity!"

Charles Castel (1658–1743), Abbé de Saint-Pierre, was a French abbot, writer and political reformer. After he had received the last rites—though only for his family's sake—he told the priest: "I am only to be reproached for this action. I do not believe a word of all this. It was a vile concession for the family and for the house, but I wanted to be the confessor of the truth all my life."

Lucilio Vanini (1584–1619) was an Italian philosopher who presumptuously called himself "Julius Caesar." Though he was ordained a Carmelite priest, he left the Catholic faith and was ultimately condemned to death as an atheist and magician. At the stake he shouted: "There is neither God nor devil: for if there were a God, I would pray him to send a thunderbolt on the council, as all that is unjust and iniquitous; and if there were a devil, I would pray him to engulf it in the subterranean regions. But since there is neither one nor the other, there is nothing for me to do."

Joseph Paul Göbbels (1897–1945) was the Nazi propaganda minister and governor of Berlin. He poisoned his children and committed suicide with his wife rather than fall into the hands of the Soviet army. Speaking of Karl Dönitz, Hitler's successor as führer of the dying Third Reich, he said: "Tell Dönitz that we understood not only how to live and fight, but also how to die."

Ernst Kaltenbrunner (1903–1946) was the Austrian-born head of the Nazi security police. One of his agents confessed at a trial that under this man's orders he had gassed three million people at the Auschwitz concentration camp. Sentenced as a war criminal to death by hanging at the Nuremburg trials, Kaltenbrunner was asked for a last statement. He replied: "I have loved my German people and my fatherland with a warm heart. I have done my duty by the laws of my people, and I am sorry my people were led this time by men who were not soldiers and that crimes were committed of which I had no knowledge."

Heinrich Himmler (1900–1945) was the German Nazi who headed the police force and supervised Hitler's death camps. When captured by the British and ordered to strip, he protested: "He does not know who I am!" When the order was repeated, he committed suicide by biting down on a vial of cyanide hidden in his mouth.

Henry IV of Germany struggled to control the church. In the course of his conflicts with Rome, he was excommunicated by the pope and at one point even set up an antipope. He died with these arrogant words: "I swear before the eye of the All-Knowing that all my efforts have been only for the advancement of my church."

Filippo Strozzi II (1489–1538), a Florentine intriguer against the Medicis, was captured by his enemies. He carved his suicide note, quoting the Latin poet Virgil, into the prison's stone wall with the tip of his sword: "If I have not known how to live, I shall know how to die. May some avenger rise from my bones!"

George Santayana (1863–1952) was a Spanish-born philosopher, poet and essayist whose relationship with religion was stormy all his life. A few days before he died of cancer after years of care by religious sisters in Rome, the nun who had quietly served him and prayed for him all that time felt obliged to say, "You are dying. You should see a priest and make your peace with God."

He replied, "Say no more of this. I shall die as I have lived."

She then asked him, "Are you suffering?"

He answered, "Not physically, but mentally."

When she asked him what he meant, he replied simply: "Desperation."

Eugene O'Neill (1888–1953), the American playwright, said a few days before he died: "When I'm dying, don't let a priest or a Protestant minister or a Salvation Army captain near me. Let me die in dignity. Keep it as simple and brief as possible. No fuss, no man of God there. If there is a God, I'll see him and we'll talk things over."

Raving just minutes before he died, he exclaimed: "I knew it! I knew it! Born in a *#&%$ hotel room and dying in a hotel room!"

Adolf Hitler (1889–1945), the infamous Nazi führer of the Third Reich, was baptized Catholic in his Austrian homeland, though he obviously apostasized as an adult. Just before he retired with his wife to a bunker beneath Berlin to commit suicide, he said to his aides: "Death for me means only freedom from worries and a very difficult life. I have been deceived by my best friends and have experienced treason. Now it has gone so far. It is finished. Good-bye."

EIGHTEEN

"That Day and Hour No One Knows"
DEATH COMES SUDDENLY

> *But about that day and*
> *hour no one knows,*
> *neither the angels of*
> *heaven, nor the Son, but*
> *only the Father.*
> —Matthew 24:36

"NOTHING IS MORE CERTAIN THAN DEATH," OBSERVED Saint Anselm, "nothing more uncertain than its hour."

We've noted in an earlier chapter that the death of a Christian is like a mini-apocalypse: for the departing individual it's the end of the world, and the Lord has come back as judge. So when Jesus said, just a few days before he died, that "no one knows" the "day and hour" of his return, the warning had a twofold meaning. The timing of his second advent in glory at the end of history is unknown to the world; and the timing of his coming for each of us—or at least for most of us—is similarly hidden.

In the final words of those for whom death comes as a surprise, the last remark is often about some trivial matter. The end arrives with no time for sad good-byes, profound observations or even one last, heartfelt prayer. Lou Costello, the beloved American actor and comedian, died after saying of his strawberry ice cream soda with two scoops: "That was the best ice-cream soda I ever tasted!" Bing Crosby dropped dead from a heart attack on a golf course in Spain after commenting: "That was a great game of golf, fellers."

Sometimes the last words are more poignant. Those about to die may attempt to reassure loved ones, and perhaps themselves, that everything is just fine. Or they may express an innocent expectation that the routine will continue, the work will be done, the loved ones will be seen again. Tomorrow seems guaranteed.

At times the irony can be quite sharp. The tyrannical King William II shouted to a member of his hunting party to kill the stag the king had missed: "Shoot, you devil! Shoot in the devil's name! Shoot, or it will be the worse for you!" The man shot, and the arrow ricocheted into the king's heart. The French philosopher Denis Diderot, warned by his wife not to eat the apricot he was holding, protested: "What possible harm could it do to me?" He ate the fruit, suffered a heart attack and dropped dead.

In each case of sudden departure we hear words that well could be our own one day, a sober warning that death continues to appear unannounced. These declarations press us to consider: how would I spend this hour if I knew it was my last?

* * *

Saint John Nepomucene Neumann (1811–1860) was the Bohemian-born Redemptorist bishop of Philadelphia. He said to a friend only hours before he dropped dead on a city sidewalk: "I feel as I never felt before. I have to go out on a little business, and the fresh air will do me good. A man must always be ready, for death comes when and where God wills it."

Paul-Louis-Charles-Marie Claudel (1868–1955) was a French diplomat, poet and dramatist. Puzzled by his symptoms, his last words were addressed to his doctor: "Do you think it could have been the sausage?"

Henri Benjamin Constant de Rebecque (1767–1830) was a French-Swiss political writer and novelist. The day he died he found himself unable to finish correcting proofs for the final volume of his *History of Religions.* He laid them aside and concluded: "The rest tomorrow."

Rudolph Valentino (1895–1926), the Italian-American star of silent film, said to someone in his sickroom: "Don't pull down the blinds! I feel fine. I want the sunlight to greet me."

Saint Frances Cabrini (1850–1917), the Italian-American founder of the Missionary Sisters of the Sacred Heart, was the first American citizen to be canonized. She died suddenly after telling one of the sisters: "Sweep the dust from the floor, especially in front of my rocker, where I will sit and receive [guests at a Christmas party]. I am a bit weary and later will rise anew."

Enrico Caruso (1873–1921), the Italian operatic tenor, died of blood poisoning after telling his wife: "Let me sleep."

John Lawrence Sullivan (1858–1918), the American boxer who was first to hold the title of heavyweight champion of the world, suffered a fatal heart attack. Before he died he told a friend: "I'll be all right in a little while."

J.R.R. Tolkien (1892–1973) was the British philologist and novelist best known for his *Lord of the Rings* trilogy. Not long before he died from pneumonia, he said to a friend: "I feel on top of the world."

Brian Oswald Donn-Byrne (1889–1928), an Irish-American novelist and journalist, died in an auto collision near his home, after announcing: "I think I'll go for a drive before dinner. Anyone come along?"

Thomas Anthony (Tommy) Dorsey (1905–1956), the popular American bandleader, said just before retiring for the night: "I plan to sleep late."

Alexandre Dumas (1824–1895), son of the author of *The Count of Monte Cristo* and a novelist and playwright himself, told his daughters: "Go and have lunch, and leave me to get some rest." When they returned he was unconscious.

Franz Joseph Haydn (1732–1809), the Austrian composer known as the "Father of the Symphony," died during the bombardment of Vienna by the armies of Napoleon. His last words to his household staff: "Children, be comforted: I am well."

Gilbert Ray Hodges (1924–1972) was a star first baseman for the Brooklyn (and later Los Angeles) Dodgers, then manager of the Washington Senators and New York Mets. Asked by one of his coaches to meet him for dinner, he answered—just seconds before dropping dead on a sidewalk—"Let's say 7:30."

Roger Eugene Maris (1934–1985) was an American baseball outfielder; playing for the New York Yankees, he set a record of sixty-one home runs in the 1961 season. Maris died of lymphatic cancer, making this last request: "I want a radio in my room."

Tullius Clinton O'Kane (1830–1912) was an American composer of sacred music. Having led the family in devotions, he concluded the Our Father with the word "Amen"—and fell dead of a heart attack.

Tyrone Power (1914–1958), the American film actor, collapsed on the set during the filming of a movie. He reassured a friend: "Don't worry. The same thing happened about a week ago."

Frank Rizzo (1920–1991), former mayor of Philadelphia who was campaigning to recapture his previous position, walked into his office and said to his secretary: "Hello, there, Jodi!" Then he went into the bathroom and dropped dead.

Jean-Baptiste-Donatien de Vimeur (1725–1807), Comte de Rochambeau, was a French general whose help secured Washington's victory over Cornwallis at Yorktown. Talking to his wife about a reception he had missed the night before because of a bad head cold, he said: "You must agree that I would have cut a pretty figure at the wedding yesterday." She left him reading and shortly returned to find him dead.

Knute Kenneth Rockne (1888–1931), the famous American football coach for the University of Notre Dame, was a late convert to the Catholic faith. He said to a fellow passenger boarding a plane: "I suggest you buy some reading material. These plane engines make an awful racket and just about shut off most conversation."

The plane crashed. His body was found with a rosary in his hands.

Francis Spellman (1889–1967), the cardinal archbishop of New York, suffered a heart attack that turned out to be fatal. As he was taken away on a stretcher, he told his doctor: "Now, don't you worry about anything."

Henri de la Tour d'Auvergne (1611–1675), Vicomte de Turenne, the marshal of France and a distinguished military leader, converted to the Catholic faith as an adult. After his officers told him to take cover in battle, he responded, only a few seconds before he was killed: "I will gladly come, for I particularly wish not to be killed just now."

Giuseppe Verdi (1813–1901) was an Italian composer of operas and sacred music. His housekeeper saw that he was buttoning up his vest in a crooked way and tried to assist him. He observed: "One button more, or one button less." Seconds later he suffered a massive stroke and fell into a coma. He died several days later.

Walter Valentino Liberace (1919–1986), the colorful American pianist and entertainer, was asked just before he died whether he wanted to go to church. He replied:

"I wish I could. I'll just stay here and watch my shows."

Charles François Gounod (1818–1893), a French composer, said to a reporter: "I know I look robust, but as Saint Paul says in his Epistle to Timothy, 'I am now ready to be offered, and the time of my departure is at hand. I have fought the good fight, I have finished the course, I have kept the faith.' I have had several attacks already. The next ..." At that moment he suffered a stroke mid-sentence. He died several days later of another stroke.

Charles Péguy (1873–1914) was a French poet who served as an officer in World War I. When one of his men protested that he didn't want to expose himself to enemy fire without a helmet, Péguy cried, "I don't have one either! Go on firing!" A few seconds later a bullet pierced Péguy's head and killed him.

Roger Touhy (1898–1959), an Irish-American mobster and bootlegger, was gunned down in Chicago soon after his release from prison. As he waited for the ambulance, he said: "I've been expecting it. The bastards never forget!"

Roberto Clemente (1934–1972) was a Puerto Rican star outfielder for the Pittsburgh Pirates. He insisted on accompanying a planeload of relief supplies for Nicaraguan earthquake victims. Just before his boarding, friends protested that the plane was unsafe, but he announced: "If you're going to die, you're going to die." The plane crashed into the sea.

John Fitzgerald Kennedy (1917–1963), thirty-fifth president of the United States, remarked in response to a comment about the dangers involved in riding in a presidential motorcade in Dallas, Texas: "If someone is going to kill me, they will kill me."

After a warm welcome from the city, the wife of the Texas governor told him as they rode in the open car: "You can't say Dallas hasn't been friendly to you."

He replied: "I certainly can't."

William O'Neill (d. 1888–1953) was an Irish-American soldier and one of Teddy Roosevelt's Rough Riders in the Spanish-American War. He declared confidently: "Sergeant, the Spanish bullet isn't made that will kill me." Moments later he was killed by a stray bullet.

Pope John Paul I (1912–1978) died in his sleep after a reign of less than a month. He had said to an aide before retiring: "Now goodnight. Until tomorrow, if God is willing."

NINETEEN

"With Me in Paradise"
DESTINY

> *Truly I tell you, today you*
> *will be with me in*
> *Paradise.*
> —Luke 23:43

IN HIS BRIEF LAST WORDS TO THE PENITENT THIEF ON the cross, Jesus made two promises. The first offered a marvelous hope: the dying man would soon be in paradise. Yet the second promise was more wonderful still: Jesus, his Savior, would be there with him.

In the final declarations of countless Catholics we find a keen awareness, a firm confidence, that they have a share in the promises our Lord made to the thief. By God's grace, they trust, their ultimate destiny will be a paradise. They speak of the life to come as a final haven, a place of rest and refreshment—even a kind of inebriation—full of joy, happiness, blessedness. They await the reward of faithfulness in this life, the glory that outweighs in its splendor all the pains and miseries suffered in this world.

Yet heaven is for them much more than a garden of delights or a crown at the end of an arduous race. They speak of it also as home: the place where they belong, where they and their loved ones will gladly return at the end of the day to meet and enjoy one another once again.

Meanwhile, their joy is multiplied by the knowledge that this new life is everlasting: once home, they will never have to leave again.

What makes heaven their home? The answer lies in the second promise to the dying thief and to all who die in God's friendship. Jesus, their elder brother, will be there with them. His mother—their mother too—will be close by. Together with all the family of the angels and saints, in heaven they will plunge at last into the depths of the love that flows between Father, Son and Holy Spirit. They have come from God, and they will return to God; he himself is their home.

Saint John beautifully summarizes the destiny of the redeemed family: "Beloved, we are God's children now; what we will be has not yet been revealed. What we do know is this: when he is revealed, we will be like him, for we will see him as he is" (1 John 3:2).

This eternal communion with God, face-to-face at last, is called the beatific vision—the vision of perfect blessedness. Human happiness knows no completion, no permanence, apart from it. Why not? Because the Creator has made men and women for himself, and they will never be fully satisfied until they experience this final divine embrace.

In fact, they will be much more than satisfied. The saints will be utterly transformed. The image of God, damaged in the Fall, will be perfectly restored in them, yes; but the culmination of their union with Christ, the God-Man, will take them higher and deeper still. They will be, as Saint Paul promises, "filled with all the fullness of God," sharing a divine life that is "abundantly far more than all we can ask or imagine" (Ephesians 3:19, 20).

Seeing him "as he is," they will become "as he is," "participants of the divine nature" (2 Peter 1:4). They will have a share of his perfections: God's own life, holiness, love, knowledge, wisdom, power, authority. What he is by nature they will become by grace.

In the meantime, as Saint John also observes, "all who have this hope in him purify themselves, just as he is pure" (1 John 3:3). Even now the glory awaiting us draws us on to finish the race (see Hebrews 12:1–2). The divine call to come home urges us to make ourselves ready for that homecoming.

A careful reflection on last words can thus strengthen and purify us, because they awaken in us a longing for our destiny in God. Once we glimpse the beauty of the ultimate destination, we will find ourselves urging our souls on toward it. The dying words of Venerable Thérèse of Saint Augustine will become our own: "Hurry! At a gallop! To paradise!"

* * *

Jeanne d'Albret (1528–1572), queen of Navarre, said to her loved ones: "Weep not for me, I pray you. God by this sickness calls me from here to enjoy a better life; and now I shall enter into the desired haven toward which this frail vessel of mine has been a long time steering."

Saint Gertrude the Great of Helfta (1256–1302), a German nun, scholar, mystic and spiritual writer, died with this prayer: "When will you come? My soul thirsts for you, O loving Father."

Frédéric Chopin clutched a crucifix to his heart and exclaimed with his last breath: "Now I am at the Source of blessedness!"

George Herman (Babe) Ruth, Jr. (1895–1948), the celebrated American baseball star, was dying of throat cancer. After being touched with a relic of Saint Frances Cabrini, he struggled to his feet. When his nurse asked where he was going, he said: "Not far. I'm just going over the valley."

After he was helped back in bed, he prayed: "My Jesus, mercy. My Jesus."

Saint Clare of Assisi died after a long illness. In her last words she addressed her own soul: "Go peacefully, because you will have good guidance on the way. Go, because he who created you and blessed you, always watching over you [as] a mother watches over her child, has also loved you tenderly."

Jacqueline Bouvier Kennedy Onassis (1929–1994) was the first lady of the United States, married to President John Fitzgerald Kennedy. As she was dying, she said of her dead children: "My little angels—I'll be with you soon."

Then she said to her living children: "Don't cry for me. I'm going to be with your father now."

Anna Maria Seton (1795–1812) was one of the first American Sisters of Charity, the order founded by her mother, Saint Elizabeth Ann Seton. Dying of tuberculosis of the bone, she said to her weeping mother: "Can it be for me? Should you not rejoice? It will be but a moment, and reunited for eternity! A happy eternity with my mother! What a thought! Laugh, Mother! Jesus!"

Ludovico Ariosto declared: "Several of my friends have already gone. I wish to see them again. And I will languish continually until I attain this happiness."

Clementine Cuvier (nineteenth century) was the daughter of the naturalist Baron Georges Cuvier. On her deathbed at the age of twenty-two, she said to a close friend: "You know we are sisters for eternity. *There* is life; it is only *there* that there is life."

Torquato Tasso (1544–1595), an Italian poet, died just before he was to be crowned poet laureate by the pope. He commented: "This is the crown with which I hoped to be crowned: not as a poet in the capital but with the glory of the blessed in heaven."

Blessed Blanche of Castile (1188–1252), queen consort of Louis VIII of France, was the mother of Saint Louis IX. At her death she prayed: "Help, you saints of God! Fly here, you angels of the Lord, and receive my soul and bear it before the All-High!"

Saint Charles Borromeo (1538–1584), Italian cardinal archbishop of Milan, was a principal figure in the Catholic Reformation and the Council of Trent. He died with the simple declaration: "Behold, Lord, I come!"

Blessed Gertrude of Delft (d. 1358) was a Dutch mystic and stigmatist who belonged to the Beguines. Dying on the Feast of the Epiphany, she sighed: "I am longing, longing to go home."

Saint Aloysius Gonzaga (1568–1591) was a Jesuit priest who died of the plague while nursing its victims in Rome. He said to the priest who was hearing his confession: "We are going, Father; we are going." The priest asked where they were going. Aloysius answered, "To heaven."

James Augustine Healy (1830–1900) was a former slave from Georgia who became the first African-American bishop in the United States, serving in Portland, Maine. At the end of a prolonged, painful illness, he replied to a query: "I wonder if heaven is worth it all? Yes! Yes! It is worth all this and infinitely more still!"

Helius Eobanus Hessus (1488–1540), a German scholar known in his time as the "King of Poets," said as he died: "I want to ascend to my Lord."

James II (1633–1701), king of England, was a Catholic convert deposed by Parliament in the famous "Glorious Revolution" of 1688. Dying in exile in France, he exclaimed to his wife: "Think of it, Madam: I am going to be happy!"

Charlotte Corday, when the executioner tried to intercept her view of the guillotine, bent forward, saying: "I have a right to be curious; I have never seen one before. It is the toilette of death, but it leads to immortality."

John McCloskey (1810–1885) was archbishop of New York and America's first cardinal. Before he lapsed into a coma, he replied to a priest friend who hoped to have the cardinal join him in Atlantic City later that year: "No, Father. I am going on a longer journey. God has been good to me all my life, and I hope he will be good enough now to take me home."

Saint Thomas Aquinas said as he lay dying from an accident: "Soon will the God of all comfort complete his mercies and fulfill my desires. Soon I shall be satisfied in him and drink of the torrents of his delights. I shall be inebriated in the abundance of his house, and in him, who is the Source, I shall behold the Light."

Servant of God Dorothy Day (1897–1980), the American journalist and social reformer who co-founded the Catholic Worker Movement, whispered: "Rise, clasp my hand, and come!"

Blessed Elizabeth of the Trinity (1880–1906), a French Carmelite and spiritual writer, said just moments before she breathed her last: "I am going to Light, to Love, to Life!"

Saint Catherine of Siena, following a stroke, prayed: "You, O Lord, call me, and I am coming to you; and I come not through my own merits but only through your mercy."

Saint Camillus de Lellis greeted his physician: "Hullo, Signor Galliano, a different Doctor is expecting me!" When asked whether he would like some refreshment, he replied: "In another quarter of an hour, I *shall* be refreshed."

Saint Francis Xavier, dying of fever on the mission field, said to those around him: "Let us all meet again at God's judgment seat."

Chiara Luce Badano said: "Don't cry for me. I'm going to Jesus. At my funeral I don't want people to cry; I want them to sing!"

Pope Saint Gregory the Great (540–604) guided the church through a troubled time as the Roman Empire was collapsing. Dying after a prolonged illness, he said: "I pray that the hand of Almighty God will raise me from the sea of this present life and let me rest on the shores of eternal life."

Venerable María Guadalupe García Zavala (1878–1963), known as Mother Lupe, was the Mexican founder of the Servants of Saint Margaret Mary and of the Poor. On her deathbed she was asked by her physician, "How are you doing, Mother Lupe?" She answered: "I'm walking toward heaven."

Stephen Kaszap (1916–1935) was a young Hungarian athlete and Jesuit novice who died of erysipelas. A priest and a nurse entered his sickroom to discover him lying unconscious, eyes open and fixed on the crucifix, with a Marian medal in his hands, having scrawled this last note: "God be with you! We will meet in heaven! Do not weep; this is my birthday in heaven. God bless you all!"

Saint Elizabeth of Hungary (1207–1231) was a Franciscan tertiary who devoted her life to serving the sick, the aged and the poor. Her last words: "This is the moment when almighty God calls his friends to himself."

Saint Pedro de San José Betancur (1626–1667), founder of the Bethlemite order, was a Franciscan tertiary from the Canary Islands who established the world's first convalescent home in the Americas, in Guatemala. In his final hours he kept repeating fervently, "Who would like to be able to see God?" Then, minutes before he died, he said, "Rejoice, let us see God."

Fulton John Sheen (1895–1979) was an American arch-bishop and pioneer of Catholic radio and television broadcasting. He said near the end of his life: "It is not that I do not love life; I do. It is just that I want to see the Lord. I have spent hours before him in the Blessed Sacrament. I have spoken to him in prayer, and about him to everyone who would listen, and now I want to see him face-to-face."

Pope John Paul II, just a few hours before slipping into a coma, said: "Let me go to the house of the Father."

Index of Names With Sources

Following is an index of people quoted in this book as well as sources for the quotes. The author has modernized some wording and punctuation.

Anre Phu Yen, Blessed, 89. Ann Ball, *Young Faces of Holiness: Modern Saints in Photos and Words* (Huntington, Ind.: Our Sunday Visitor, 2004), p. 220.

Anselm of Canterbury, Saint, 21, 176. Le Comte, p. 8

Anthony of Padua, Saint, 112, 150. Alice Curtayne, *St. Anthony of Padua* (Chicago: Franciscan Herald, 1932), p. 104; Sophronius Clasen, *St. Anthony: Doctor of the Gospel,* Ignatius Brady, trans. (Chicago: Franciscan Herald, 1961), p. 210.

Antoninus of Florence, Saint, 77. Alban Bulter, *The Lives of the Fathers, Martyrs and Other Principal Saints,* volume 5 (New York: D. & J. Sadlier, 1864), http://www.ewtn.com/library/MARY/STANTONI.HTM.

Antony the Great, Saint, 128. Le Comte, p. 9.

Apphianus, Saint, 83. Ruffin, *Last Words,* p. 17.

Aquinas, Saint Thomas, 12, 124, 133, 151, 191. Raïssa Maritain, *St. Thomas Aquinas: The Angel of the Schools,* Julie Kernan trans. (New York: Sheed & Ward, 1955), p. 113; Ruffin, *Last Words,* p. 17; Mary Fabyan Windeatt, *Saint Thomas Aquinas: The Story of "The Dumb Ox"* (Rockford, Ill.: TAN, 1993), p. 69.

Aretino, Pietro, 98. Le Comte, p. 10.

Ariosto, Ludovico, 37, 189. Laura Ward, *Famous Last Words: The Ultimate Collection of Finales and Farewells* (London: Chrysalis Books Group, 2004), p. 21; Ruffin, *Last Words,* p. 17.

Arnould, Sophie, 162. Claude Aveline, *Les Mots de la Fin* (Paris: Hachette, 1957), p. 253, as quoted in Ruffin, *Last Words,* p. 18.

Augustine, Saint, 110. Aveline, p. 188, as quoted in Ruffin, *Last Words,* p. 19.

Babylas, Saint, 106. Lockyer, p. 141.

Badano, Chiara Luce, 27, 192. Ann Ball, *Young Faces of Holiness,* p. 23.

Balzac, Honoré de, 17. Ruffin, *Last Words,* p. 21.

Barrymore, John, 96. L. Ward, p. 44.

Bastiat, Claude-Frédéric, 74, 164. Stanislas A. Lortie. "Claude-Frédéric Bastiat", Susan Birkenseer trans. (The Catholic Encyclopedia Online Edition, 2005) http://newadvent.org/cathen/02345b.htm; Le Comte, p. 18.

Baudelaire, Charles, 76. Ruffin, *Last Words,* p. 22.

Boileau, Nicolas, 13. Green, p. 61.

Boleyn, Anne, 95. Ruffin, *Last Words*, p. 15.

Bonaparte, Elisabeth Patterson, 98. Le Comte, p. 26.

Bonaparte, Pauline, 168. Ruffin, *Last Words*, p. 30.

Borgia, Cesare, 161. L. Ward, p. 98.

Borgia, Lucrezia, 29. Le Comte, p. 27.

Bossuet, Bishop Jacques-Bénigne, 72. Ruffin, *Last Words*, p. 31.

Bouhours, Dominique, 14. Le Comte, p. 28.

Boulanger, Lili, 127. Leonie Rosenstiel, *Nadia Boulanger* (New York: Norton, 1982), p. 135, as quoted in Ruffin, *Last Words*, p. 32.

Brandsma, Servant of God Titus, 134. Ball, *Modern Saints*, p. 371.

Braun Hitler, Eva, 129. Ruffin, *Last Words*, p. 96.

Bridget of Sweden, Saint, 104. Ruffin, *Last Words*, p. 32.

Bruce, King Robert, 12. Le Comte, p. 32.

Bruyère, Élisabeth, 58. O'Malley, *Saints of North America*, p. 140.

Cajetan of Thiene, Saint, 58. Herbert Thurston and Donald Attwater, *Butler's Lives of the Saints*, volume 3 (Westminster, Md.: Newman, 1956), p. 273, as quoted in Ruffin, *Last Words*, p. 39.

Calderón, Rodrigo, 170. Green, p. 71.

Camacho, Servant of God Maria de la Luz, 89. Joan Carroll Cruz, *Saintly Women of Modern Times* (Huntington, Ind.: Our Sunday Visitor, 2004), p. 144.

Camillus de Lellis, Saint, 38, 54, 113, 192. C.C. Martindale, *Life of Saint Camillus* (New York: Sheed & Ward, 1946), pp. 143–144, 151; Alban Goodier, *Saints for Sinners* (New York: Image, 1959), p. 108.

Capone, Al, 64. L. Ward, p. 153.

Carême, Antoine, 21. Green, p. 80.

Carroll, Charles, 112, 117. Kate Mason Rowland, *The Life of Charles Carroll of Carrollton* (New York: Putnam, 1898), pp. 368–370, as quoted in Ruffin, *Last Words*, pp. 40–41.

Caruso, Enrico, 179. Ruffin, *Last Words*, p. 41.

Castel, Charles, 172. Le Comte, p. 183.

Catherine Labouré, Saint, 155. Ruffin, *Last Words*, p. 113.

Catherine of Aragon, 48. "Letter of Katharine of Aragon to her hus-

Chi Zhuze, Saint, 5. Ball, *Young Faces of Holiness,* p. 177.

Chopin, Frédéric, 29, 42, 55, 131, 188. James Huneker, *Chopin: the Man and His Music* (New York: Scribner, 1899), p. 49, as quoted in Ruffin, *Last Words,* p. 46; Lockyer, p. 118; Le Comte, p. 48.

Clare of Assisi, 4, 150, 188. Fra' Tommaso da Celano, *The Life of St. Clare Virgin* (Assisi: Editrice Minerva, 2004), p. 76–77.

Claudel, Paul-Louis-Charles-Marie, 178. L. Ward, p. 34.

Clement XI, Pope, 117. Ludwig von Pastor, *A History of the Popes,* volume 33 (St. Louis: Herder, 1941), p. 533, as quoted in Ruffin, *Last Words,* p. 48.

Clement XII, Pope, 168. Alexis François Artaud de Montor, *The Lives of the Roman Pontiffs,* volume 2 (New York: Catholic Publication Society of America, 1897), p. 264, as quoted in Ruffin, *Last Words,* p. 48.

Clement XIV, Pope, 40. de Montor, p. 376, as quoted in Ruffin, *Last Words,* pp. 48–49.

Clemente, Roberto, 183. Ruffin, *Last Words,* p. 49.

Collins, Dominic, 87. H. Patrick Montague, *The Saints and Martyrs of Ireland* (Buckinghamshire, England: Colin Smythe, 1981), p. 82.

Columba, Saint, 146. Lucy Menzies, *St. Columba of Iona: A Short Account of His Life* (Glasgow: Iona Community, 1974), p. 131.

Columbus, Christopher, 104. Ruffin, *Last Words,* p. 50.

Comte, Auguste, 169. Ruffin, *Last Words,* p. 51.

Conan Doyle, Sir Arthur, 135. Ruffin, *Last Words,* p. 51.

Connelly, Cornelia, 108. Anonymous, *Life of Cornelia Connelly* (London: Longmons, Green, 1922), p. 469, as quoted in Ruffin, *Last Words,* p. 51.

Constant de Rebecque, Henri Benjamin, 178. Le Comte, p. 54.

Cooke, Terence Cardinal, 13. O'Malley, *Saints of North America,* pp. 389–390.

Cooper, Gary, 30. Ruffin, *Last Words,* p. 52.

Corday, Charlotte, 135, 191. Le Comte, p. 55; L. Ward, p. 68.

Corot, Jean-Baptiste-Camille, 11. Ruffin, *Last Words,* p. 52.

Cortusio, Lodovico, 97. Michelle Lovric. *Weird Wills & Eccentric Last Wishes* (New York: Barnes & Noble, 2000), p. 19; Robert S. Menchin, *Where There's a Will* (New York: toExcel, 2000), p. 150.

Francis of Paola, Saint, 65. Gino J. Simi and Mario M. Segreti, *Saint Francis of Paola: God's Miracle Worker Supreme (1416–1507)* (Rockford, Ill.: TAN, 1977), p. 187.

Francis Solano, Saint, 112. Mary Fabyan Windeatt, *Saint Francis Solano: Wonder-Worker of the New World and Apostle of Argentina and Peru* (Rockford, Ill.: TAN, 1994), p. 213.

Francis Xavier, Saint, 106, 141, 192. Goodier, p. 75; Ruffin, *Last Words*, p. 75; Henri Daniel-Rops, *The Heroes of God* (New York: Echo, 1965), p. 89.

Franco, Francisco, 98. L. Ward, p. 101.

Frank, Hans, 66. L. Ward, 61; Kingsbury Smith, "The Execution of Nazi War Criminals," October 16, 1946, International News Service, http://members. tripod.com/neal_ford/nuremberg.html.

Galois, Evariste, 163. Ruffin, *Last Words*, p. 77.

Gambetta, Léon-Michel de, 130. Le Comte, p. 86.

Garcia, Gloria María Elizondo, 145. O'Malley, *Saints of North America*, p. 477.

Gardiner, Stephen, 161. Le Comte, p. 87.

Gemma Galgani, Saint, 41, 141. "St. Gemma's Last Illness and Heroic Death," http://www.stgemma.com/eng_death.html; Ruffin, *Last Words*, p. 77.

Genoveffa De Trois, Venerable, 31. Cruz, p. 103.

Gertrude of Delft, Blessed, 190. Ruffin, *Last Words*, p. 80.

Gertrude the Great of Helfta, Saint, 188. Ruffin, *Last Words*, p. 80.

Getulius, Saint, 106. Ruffin, *Last Words*, p. 80.

Ghebre Michael, Blessed, 73. O'Malley, *Saints of Africa*, p. 122.

Gianna Berretta Molla, 4. Cruz, p. 113.

Gibbons, James, 153. Ruffin, *Last Words*, pp. 80–81.

Gilbert of Sempringham, Saint, 122. Ruffin, *Last Words*, p. 81.

Giustiniani, Lorenzo, 58. Ruffin, *Last Words*, p. 81.

Gleason, Jackie, 100. Ruffin, *Last Words*, p. 81.

Goar, Saint, 152. Green, p. 116.

Göbbels, Joseph Paul, 173. Ralf George Reuth, *Goebbels* (New York: Morrow, 1989), pp. 509–510, as quoted in Ruffin, *Last Words*, p. 82.

Godwin, 169. Le Comte, p. 90.

Kaltenbrunner, Ernst, 173. Smith, "Execution," http://members. tripod.com/neal_ford/nuremberg.html.

Kaszap, Stephen, 193. Ball, *Young Faces of Holiness,* p. 147.

Kennedy, John Fitzgerald, 183. Ruffin, *Last Words,* 110.

Kilmer, Joyce, 32. Robert Cortes Holliday, ed., *Joyce Kilmer* (Port Washington, N.Y.: Kennikat, 1918), p. 109.

Knox, Ronald, 57. Ruffin, *Last Words,* p. 112.

Laharpe, Jean-François de, 111. Ruffin, *Last Words,* p. 113.

Lamballe, Marie-Thérèse-Luise de Savoie-Carignan, 18. Ruffin, *Last Words,* pp. 113–114.

Laplace, Pierre Simon, 55. Le Comte, p. 131.

Lawrence, Saint, 95. Ruffin, *Last Words,* p. 115.

LeCouvreur, Adrienne, 172. Le Comte, p. 133.

Lekeu, Guillame, 11. David Ewen, *Composers of Yesterday* (New York: Wilson, 1937), p. 247, as quoted in Ruffin, *Last Words,* p. 117.

Leo X, Pope, 144. Charles L. Mee, *White Robe, Black Robe* (New York: Putnam, 1972), p. 288, as quoted in Ruffin, *Last Words,* p. 117.

Leo XI, Pope, 37. de Montor, volume 1, p. 931, as quoted in Ruffin, *Last Words,* p. 117.

Lewis, George, 131. Tom Bethell, *George Lewis* (Berkeley, Calif.: University of California Press, 1977), p. 275, as quoted in Ruffin, *Last Words,* pp. 117–118.

Liberace, Walter Valentino, 182. Bob Thomas, *Liberace: The True Story* (New York: St. Martin, 1987), p. 269, as quoted in Ruffin, *Last Words,* p. 118.

Lieutaud, Joseph, 99. Le Comte, p. 136.

Liguori, Saint Alphonsus, 140. Ruffin, *Last Words,* p. 118.

Lombardi, Vince, 11, 131. Michael O'Brien, *Vince: A Personal Biography of Vince Lombardi* (New York: Morrow, 1987), pp. 373–374, as quoted in Ruffin, *Last Words,* p. 119.

Long, Mary Ann, 75. Ball, *Modern Saints,* p. 412.

Louis I the Pious, Emperor, 49. Le Comte, p. 138.

Louis VI, King, 123. Aveline, p. 190, as quoted in Ruffin, *Last Words,* p. 120.

Louis VIII, King, 75. Joy Law, *Fleur de Lys* (New York: McGraw-Hill,

Mozart, Wolfgang Amadeus, 156. Le Comte, p. 154.

Murat, Joachim, 170. Le Comte, p. 155.

Murphy, Frank, 74. Ruffin, *Last Words,* p. 141.

Napoleon Bonaparte, 74. Menchin, p. 128.

Narváez, Ramón María, 172. L. Ward, p. 100.

Nerinckx, Charles, 119. O'Malley, *Saints of North America,* p. 372.

Neumann, Saint John Nepomucene, 178. Michael J. Curley, *Bishop John Neumann, C.SS.R: Fourth Bishop of Philadelphia.* (Philadelphia: Bishop Neumann Center, 1952), p. 394.

Newman, Venerable John Henry, 39. Meriol Trevor, *Newman, Light in Winter* (Garden City, N.Y.: Doubleday, 1963), pp. 642, 645, as quoted in Ruffin, *Last Words,* p. 143.

Nicholas, Saint, 104. Le Comte, p. 157.

Nicolas, Sebastien-Roch, 43. Le Comte, p. 46.

Nicolini, Venerable Galileo, 151. Ball, *Young Faces of Holiness,* p. 84.

Noah Mawaggali, Saint, 88. Ball, *Modern Saints,* p. 91.

Nostradame, Michel de (Nostradamus), 155. "Biography of Nostradamus." http://www.activemind.com/Mysterious/Topics/Nostradamus/biography.html.

O'Carolan, Turlough, 22. Le Comte, p. 42.

O'Daly, Thaddeus, 86. Montague, p. 79.

O'Kane, Tullius Clinton, 180. Jacob H. Hall, *Biography of Gospel Song and Hymn Writers* (Chicago: Revell, 1914), p. 63, as quoted in Ruffin, *Last Words,* p. 145.

Onassis, Jacqueline Bouvier Kennedy, 188. *The Globe* and *The National Enquirer,* June 7, 1994, as quoted in Ruffin, *Last Words,* p. 146.

O'Neill, Eugene, 175. Ruffin, *Last Words,* p. 146.

O'Neill, William, 184. L. Ward, p. 111.

Pambo, Saint, 56. O'Malley, *Saints of Africa,* p. 95.

Pantellini, Sister Teresa Valse, 116. Ball, *Modern Saints,* p. 201.

Parater, Servant of God Frank, 158. O'Malley, *Saints of North America,* p. 61.

Pascal, Blaise, 63. Green, p. 112.

Patrick, Saint, 57. Paul Gallico, *The Steadfast Man: A Biography of St. Patrick* (New York: Doubleday, 1958), p. 150.

Pirandello, Luigi, 153. Gaspare Giudice, *Pirandello* (London: Oxford University Press, 1975), p. 206, as quoted in Ruffin, *Last Words,* p. 154.

Pius V, Pope Saint, 28. Robin Anderson, *St. Pius V: A Brief Account of His Life, Times, Virtues and Miracles* (Rockford, Ill.: TAN, 1989), p. 92.

Pius VI, Pope, 50. Pastor, p. 388, as quoted in Ruffin, *Last Words,* p. 155.

Pius IX, Pope, 111. Ruffin, *Last Words,* p. 155.

Pius X, Pope Saint, 28, 40, 109, 132. F.A. Forbes, *Pope St. Pius X* (Rockford, Ill.: TAN, 1987), pp. 119, 121; Katherine Burton, *The Great Mantle: The Life of Giuseppe Melchiore Sarto, Pope Pius X* (New York: Longmans, Green, 1950), p. 221; Green, p. 142; Ruffin, *Last Words,* pp. 155–156.

Pius XI, Pope, 31. *New York Times,* February 10, 1939, as quoted in Ruffin, *Last Words,* p. 156.

Pius XII, Pope, 110. Philip S. Land, "How Pius XII Died," *America,* November 8, 1958, p. 163, as quoted in Ruffin, *Last Words,* p. 156.

Pizarro, Francisco, 68. Le Comte, p. 169; Ruffin, *Last Words,* p. 156.

Poisson, Jeanne Antoinette (Marquise de Pompadour), 170. Robinson, p. 173.

Polycarp, Saint, 80. Author's adaptation from "The Martyrdom of Polycarp" in Roberts and Donaldson, volume 1, p. 41.

Polycronius, Saint, 86. Ruffin, *Last Words,* p. 157.

Pope, Alexander, 101, 121. L. Ward, p. 21; Le Comte, p. 170.

Power, Tyrone, 180. Fred Lawrence Guiles, *Tyrone Power* (Garden City, N.Y.: Doubleday, 1979), p. 305, as quoted in Ruffin, *Last Words,* p. 159.

Protasius, Saint, 50. Green, p. 118.

Puccini, Giacomo, 116. Ruffin, *Last Words,* p. 159.

Pulaski, Casimir, 138. Sally Fitzgerald, "Root and Branch: O'Connor of Georgia," *Georgia Historical Society,* volume 64 (1980), p. 13.

Quezon, Manuel Luis, 18. Ruffin, *Last Words,* p. 160.

Quinault, Philippe, 4. Guthke, p. 4.

Rabelais, François, 95, 165. Lovric, p. 17; Le Comte, p. 174.

Racine, Jean, 32, 74. Ruffin, *Last Words,* p. 161.

Rameau, Jean-Phillipe, 168. Ruffin, *Last Words,* p. 161.

Sarsfield, Patrick, 17. Le Comte, p. 185.

Savio, Saint Dominic, 152. Peter Lappin, *Dominic Savio: Teenage Saint* (Fort Collins, Col.: Roman Catholic, 1954), p. 133.

Saxe, Maurice, Comte de, 165. Ruffin, *Last Words,* p. 172.

Scarron, Paul, 19. Ruffin, *Last Words,* p. 172.

Schmitt, Aloysius, 136. L. Ward, p. 109.

Serra, Junípero, 42, 145. Le Comte, p. 188; Ruffin, *Last Words,* p. 174.

Seton, Anna Maria, 189. Ruffin, *Last Words,* p. 174.

Seton, Saint Elizabeth Ann, 111, 138. Ruffin, *Last Words,* p. 175; Le Comte, p. 188.

Seyss-Inquart, Artur, 162. Smith, "Execution."

Shave Head, 72. Robert M. Utley, *The Lance and the Shield* (New York: Holt, 1993), p. 305, as quoted in Ruffin, *Last Words,* p. 175.

Sheed, Frank, 100. Wilfred Sheed, *Frank and Maisie: A Memoir with Parents* (New York: Simon and Schuster, 1985), p. 286, as quoted in Ruffin, *Last Words,* p. 176.

Sheen, Archbishop Fulton J., 194. Eulogy by Archbishop Edward T. O'Meara, December 13, 1979, epilogue of Fulton J. Sheen, *Treasure in Clay: The Autobiography of Fulton J. Sheen* (San Francisco: Ignatius, 1980), p. 354.

Sherman, William Tecumseh, 171. John F. Marszalek, *Sherman: A Soldier's Passion for Order* (New York: Free Press, 1993), p. 492, as quoted in Ruffin, *Last Words,* p. 176.

Sinatra, Frank, 42. Robinson, p. 161.

Sinclair, Maggie, 33. Ball, *Faces of Holiness II,* p. 194.

Socrates, 2. Plato, *Phaedo,* 118a.

Solanus Casey, Venerable, 31. Michael Crosby, *Solanus Casey: The Official Account of a Virtuous American Life* (New York: Crossroad, 2000), p. 145.

Spellman, Francis Cardinal, 181. John Cooney, *The American Pope* (New York: Dell, 1984), p. 325, as quoted in Ruffin, *Last Words,* p. 179.

Stanislaw I, King, 99. Le Comte, p. 194.

Stankovik, Maria, 32. Cruz, p. 156.

Staub, Marie-Clément, 143. O'Malley, *Saints of North America,* p. 469.

Stolberg-Stolberg, Friedrich Leopold, Count von, 39. Ruffin, *Last Words,* p. 182.

Tolkien, J.R.R., 179. Daniel Grotta, *The Biography of J.R.R. Tolkien* (Philadelphia: Running, 1977), p. 253, as quoted in Ruffin, *Last Words,* p. 191.

Toscanini, Aturo, 19. Ruffin, *Last Words,* p. 192.

Touhy, Roger, 183. Ruffin, *Last Words,* p. 192.

Toulouse-Lautrec, Henri, 101. Ruffin, *Last Words,* p. 192.

Tour d'Auvergne, Henri de la, 182. Ruffin, *Last Words,* p. 193.

Toussaint, Pierre, 36. Arthur and Elizabeth Odell Sheehan, *Pierre Toussaint* (New York: Kennedy, 1955), p. 229, as quoted in Ruffin, *Last Words,* p. 192.

Tremblay, François-Joseph le Clerc du, 106. Le Comte, p. 133.

Trouvé of Saint Ann, Blessed Richard, 90. O'Malley, *Saints of North America,* p. 330.

Turgot, Anne-Robert-Jacques, 19. Ruffin, *Last Words,* p. 193.

Umberto II, King, 16. Ruffin, *Last Words,* p. 99.

Valentino, Rudolph, 178. Le Comte, p. 207.

Vallée, Rudy, 21. Ruffin, *Last Words,* pp. 194–195.

Vanini, Lucilio, 173. Le Comte, p. 207.

Vercillis, Comtesse de, 102. Robinson, p. 82.

Verdi, Giuseppe, 182. Ruffin, *Last Words,* pp. 195–196.

Verne, Jules, 113. Ruffin, *Last Words,* p. 196.

Vianney, Saint Jean-Marie-Baptiste, 114. Mary Fabyan Windeatt, *The Curé of Ars: The Story of Saint John Vianney, Patron Saint of Parish Priests* (Rockford, Ill.: TAN, 1991), p. 209; Francis Trochu, *The Curé of Ars: St. Jean-Marie-Baptiste Vianney,* Ernest Graf, trans. (Rockford, Ill.: TAN, 1977), p. 36.

Villa, Poncho, 1. Guthke, p. 10.

Villars, Claude-Louis-Hector, Duke of, 20. Ruffin, *Last Words,* pp. 196–197.

Vimeur, Jean-Baptiste-Donatien de, 181. Ruffin, *Last Words,* p. 166.

Vincent de Paul, Saint, 27, 68. Mary Purcell, *The World of Monsieur Vincent* (Chicago: Loyola University Press, 1989), p. 229; Theodore Maynard, *Apostle of Charity: The Life of St. Vincent de Paul* (London: Catholic Book Club, 1941), p. 311.

Voltaire, 99, 171. Guthke, p. 6; Ruffin, *Last Words,* p. 197.